Augsburg College
George Sverdrup Library
Minneapolis, Minnesota 55404

Ward Number Six

Ward Number Six

David Lebedoff

CHARLES SCRIBNER'S SONS • NEW YORK

Copyright © 1972 David Lebedoff

This book published simultaneously in the
United States of America and in Canada—
Copyright under the Berne Convention

All rights reserved. No part of this book
may be reproduced in any form without the
permission of Charles Scribner's Sons.

A-1.72 [c]

Printed in the United States of America
Library of Congress Catalog Card Number 70-37181
SBN 684-12823-3 (Trade cloth)

To my brother jonathan

A convenient philosophy . . . do nothing, and your conscience is clear, and you feel you are wise. . . . No, sir, it is not philosophy, it is not breadth of vision, but laziness, fakerism, drowsy stupefaction. . . .

ANTON CHEKOV
Ward No. Six

Ward Number Six

1

Bill Mullin only phones me for two reasons, lunch or money, so when I took his call I couldn't help but note, with mild alarm, that it was already quite late in the afternoon.

Of course, when Bill asks for money it's not for himself. He has a number of causes, the most expensive for me being the Minnesota Democratic-Farmer-Labor party. And at that time —late summer 1967—he was the Hennepin County DFL Chairman. The county organization was almost always in debt. There was no chance that Bill's call was purely social.

"Dave," he began, "we're really in a bind."

The plural pronoun was ominous. The last time Bill was in a bind, I'd ended up peddling twenty tickets to a benefit performance at the Tyrone Guthrie Theatre. The inducements, by our county standards, were just fine—*The House of Atreus,* followed by a champagne reception with Hubert Humphrey and Sir Tyrone—but even so I'd had to work a week to meet my quota. Political donations aren't tax deductible.

"Say, Bill, I'm kind of busy right now. Can I call you back sometime? Maybe we can have lunch."

"Listen," he said, 'it so happens that this has nothing to do with contributions. Just relax and listen."

I relaxed and listened. What Bill had in mind was free, but puzzling. He wanted me to run for chairman of my ward club. "*Our* ward club," he emphasized, with a further feint at grammatical involvement, but not inaccurately since Bill and I are neighbors. The old chairman was moving out of the ward and there was no one to take his place. I was assured that the job entailed scarcely any work. Just chairing a meeting once a month.

My first reaction was simple embarrassment. I had no idea what Bill was talking about. I hated to admit it, but I wasn't really sure which ward I lived in. A few months earlier, when moving into my new apartment, I had been vaguely aware of moving *out* of the Fifth Ward, and it now occurred to me that I must have moved *into* some other ward as well. But I'd never given the matter any thought. There being no way to bluff it, I confessed my ignorance to Bill.

"The Sixth Ward," he said patiently, "and don't worry about not knowing anyone there. It really isn't much of a club. It's a blue-collar neighborhood, you know, and very few people go to meetings. But it'll look terrible if there's no chairman."

"What makes you think they'd vote for me?"

"Oh, say, that's no problem. I know a couple of these guys from our county meetings. And you and I and your brother are three votes. Around here, that's a real bloc. Anyway, I'm sure there won't be any opposition. Come on."

"I don't know, Bill. Let me think it over."

I really was tempted. My relief that the call hadn't cost me anything had left me with a general sense of well-being. I reflected that it might be pleasant to enjoy a title without much attendant responsibility.

At the same time, I knew that Bill's call was based on a misunderstanding. He thought I was a politician, a "political activist" as he put it. And I was no such thing, though I could see where he'd received that impression—I'd just returned to Minneapolis from a year in Washington as an aide to Senator Mondale, on whose staff I'd practiced law when he was Attorney General of Minnesota. I couldn't blame Bill for thinking that anyone who had spent so much time around politicians was something of a politician himself. I'd often had the same thought. The problem was that to politicians, I was a lawyer. When they thought of me, they thought of research. So finally I'd come back to Minneapolis and the practice of law. Since I'd been back, though, I'd been meaning to get involved in the DFL party at the grass-roots level. Hence my sporadic ticket selling. And now I was being offered the chairmanship of a ward. About which I knew nothing. So during the next week, by dint of many questions, each carefully couched to conceal any personal interest, I found out quite a bit about the Sixth Ward.

The city of Minneapolis is politically divided into thirteen wards, and though each has some distinctive characteristics, the Sixth is in many respects unique. It is geographically very large, but populated only at its fringes, the center of the area being occupied by downtown Minneapolis and its ring of warehouses and flour mills. The residential population of the ward is concentrated at its eastern extremity, near the West Bank of the Mississippi River. This is the oldest area of the city. The houses are small and run down, and much of the population is poor, transient, and elderly.

I was told that things were changing, though. The University of Minnesota, cramped for space and faced with a spiraling enrollment, was starting to expand its campus onto the West Bank of the river. Two large classroom buildings and a library had already been built. For the time being, students had to find their own housing. They spread out all over the West Bank, moving into aging wooden duplexes, finding space above stores, in attics, in garages.

It was impossible for the Dean of Students to regulate this new dispersed populace, and so he didn't even try. I found this fact remarkable. When I was an undergraduate at the University of Minnesota, ten years earlier, even the commuters found their lives very closely regulated by the Dean and his one-hundred-man staff. But the official attitude toward the West Bank had from the start been one of laissez faire. Accordingly, the area attracted those least receptive to dormitories and rules.

Some of these students, I was told, were active in politics. In 1966, they had tried to take over the Sixth Ward DFL Club, and though their attempt had failed, a few of them did manage to be sent as delegates to the DFL state convention later that year. It was assumed that they would try again. I found myself hoping so, since, with a warm and expanding glow of ambition, I had gradually decided to run for the ward chairmanship and still thought of myself as young enough to garner student allies.

But that's as far as my strategy got, for before I'd had a chance to convey my availability to Bill, *he* called *me* to announce that he had another candidate for the chairmanship and that he hoped I'd understand. He explained that when he called before, he hadn't realized that Virgil Moline was interested. Virgil, an official of the school janitors' union, was an old-time member of the ward club. He knew the local people and would be a stronger candidate than I. Strength might be necessary, since Bill had heard a rumor that some of the students were going to try again to get one of their own number elected.

I consoled myself with the thought that at least I hadn't openly tried to accept Bill's offer before he withdrew it, and I managed to convey the thought that my decision would in any case have been negative. But if the slight to my pride was thus minimized, I remained somewhat rankled with Bill's handling of the matter until, several days later, I realized that the ward election was scheduled for an evening when I had to be in New York anyway. Not without a sense of satisfaction, I let Bill know that I couldn't even be there to vote for Virgil Moline.

I returned from New York the night after the election. (The Sixth Ward DFL Club meets on the first Monday of every month.) My brother immediately filled me in on what had happened. He couldn't get over it. Bill had called around dinnertime to remind him of the election, and later they had walked over together to the meeting, which is usually held in the Mayor's Reception Room at the Minneapolis City Hall, only a few blocks from our apartment house. Because Bill had taken a nap and overslept, they didn't arrive until just before eight o'clock, the scheduled meeting time. When they entered the meeting room they found the place was jammed. Every chair was taken. People were standing against the walls. And most of them were young. The students, it seems, were out in force, and the first order of business was a challenge to their right to vote. The ward club constitution, of which Bill had one of the few copies, required that no one could vote in a ward election unless he had attended a previous meeting and paid one dollar annual dues. This requirement did disqualify a certain number of students, but it disenfranchised others as well, such as my brother and a rather surprising number of the older party regulars, too, including, it should be noted, Bill.

Then someone moved that the vote be restricted to those over twenty-one. The debate on this was predictably fierce, but the motion finally failed. Anyone over eighteen could participate. That settled it; the students took over the club. By a margin of about ten votes, they captured all the ward offices. Not just the chairmanship, all the offices.

According to my brother, this wasn't so bad. The new chairman was very impressive at first glance. His name was Vance Opperman, and my brother reported that he was very smooth. He was a second-year law student at the University. I'd always believed that young people should participate directly in politics rather than waste their time in the youth auxiliaries that both parties maintain, so this student takeover seemed to augur well. And there was the very soothing reflection that it had been Moline, not me, who had been beaten. I had no connection with the defeat at all. So I wouldn't have to feel uncomfortable at the next ward club meeting, which I now definitely planned to attend.

I was looking forward to it. Some years back I had attended

a few meetings of my old ward club, the locally infamous Fifth, but that was a bastion of what is now called the Old Politics; and, since I was one of the younger and (no trick) more liberal members, I never felt that I was getting anywhere. The new club promised to be considerably better. Besides, this was going to be an interesting year politically. The war in Vietnam was becoming quite an issue. Everyone had been talking and arguing about it for some time, but now the focus was more directly political. The DFL State Central Committee had held a heated debate on its Vietnam resolution before finally commending the Administration. A new group called the Dissenting Democrats had opened an office three doors down from the DFL headquarters. And one day I saw in the paper that some Minnesotans whose names I didn't recognize had actually asked our senior Senator, Eugene McCarthy, to let them use his name as a presidential candidate in opposition to the war. They claimed to have spoken to McCarthy about this, and he had "not discouraged" their efforts. I remember my surprise at seeing that story halfway down the front page of the Minneapolis *Star*. I'd met McCarthy a number of times and during my year in Washington had spent some time over at his office. In fact, since McCarthy was frequently absent, I remembered that office better than I did the man. It had more style than the quarters of his colleagues: dark gray walls, indirect lighting, real books. Cloistered, but elegant. How could the occupant of that office lend his name to this harebrained scheme? I was sure he'd been misquoted.

The weeks passed, I was busy, and soon it was time for my first meeting of the Sixth Ward Club. Bill Mullin, plucky in defeat, phoned twice to remind me, but I'd already marked the date on my calendar. I was anxious to take part in the rejuvenated club. The three of us—Bill, my brother Jon, and I—arrived at the meeting somewhat early, about a quarter to eight.

I'll never forget walking in that door. Several dozen students were already there and at our entrance they turned toward us a collective stare of such intense hostility that even now that memory chills. I couldn't understand it. What had I done? As we made our way past angry, silent and astonishingly youthful faces, it gradually became apparent that my sin consisted of close proximity to Bill Mullin. Poor Bill, then thirty-three, was very clearly in the students' eyes the living symbol of Old Guard venality. He graciously acknowledged the obvious by whispering that perhaps Jon and I would be better off if we didn't sit too near him. In full agreement but absurdly loyal, we stuck by the hapless leper. We found three empty seats at the back of the room, and from this purdah I was able to look the place over.

Not everyone there was young, but we three appeared to be the only ones present between the ages of twenty-five and sixty. So far as the Sixth Ward Club was concerned, the generation gap was more like a canyon. There was even segregated seating. The older members, looking none too friendly themselves, were all together in one corner, across the aisle from us. The students outnumbered them about two-to-one and occupied the rest of the hall. For the most part, their appearance was unexceptional. A few were dressed in what by Minneapolis standards is full hippie regalia. No one was barefoot—this was late autumn in Minnesota—but one fellow did sport a string of cowbells. The tonsorial norm was far from alarming, and some of the girls were good-looking. The only far-out figure in sight was a young man who resembled a sort of Fauve Christ. His dark hair flowed a good foot past his shoulders, and his moustache was spectacular. All of the older people were looking at him, but he was looking at us, and Bill squirmed in his chair.

I was uncomfortable myself. I still couldn't get over the fact that the students very obviously didn't like us. It was a rude awakening. It wasn't fair. I was not yet thirty, I deserved to be trusted.

These reflections were interrupted by a tap on my shoulder and, turning, I found one of the pretty young girls I'd noticed earlier, a dark and smiling charmer who, to my surprise, was greeting me by name. She introduced herself as Katy, and then proceeded most engagingly to remind me that I knew her. She explained that her mother had been active in St. Paul politics and used to visit the Attorney General's office, daughter in tow, when I had worked there years before. I began to recall the mother, and her daughter, too, who still looked about fifteen. I was intensely grateful for her friendliness in that harshly disaffected crowd. We chatted awhile and then she brought over and introduced a shy, somewhat less friendly, young man named Joel, who looked scarcely older than Katy and turned out to be her husband. I'd never felt so old in my life. I'd never felt *old* before. It was no longer possible to think of the students as near contemporaries. There was no doubt about it, I was getting there.

At precisely eight o'clock the meeting was called to order. The new Chairman, Vance Opperman, was presiding. He was a big, good-looking fellow, of commanding presence, but his physical appearance seemed to suggest a factional compromise. From head to toe, there was, politically speaking, something for everyone in that room. His long blond hair and cowboy boots were surely a link to the youthful constituency that had elected him Chairman. The sharkskin suit and red plaid vest might have been meant to mollify the oldsters, who were themselves in shirtsleeves. Certainly his opening remarks were conciliatory. He dealt at some length with the need for all of us to work together for the good of the party. I agreed, but frankly I didn't think the crowd was with him.

The meeting was being devoted to a discussion of the war in Vietnam. Resolutions would be entertained, but the preliminary bout was a debate between two professors from the University of Minnesota, each limited by the chair to a ten-minute presentation. A professor of political science defended the Administration position in Vietnam, and a professor of mathematics attacked it. I was opposed to the war, but it was clear that the political science professor was the superior advocate. He spoke simply and well, though toward the end he lost most of the audience by referring to the Soviets as "Ruskies." I was very disappointed with the mathematician. He rambled on in a squeaky voice, and I was irritated by his almost total reliance on emotion when there was such a broad deep pool of fact and reason into which he might have dipped.

Following the debate, resolutions from the floor were entertained. There was only one; it had been mimeographed before the meeting, and as it was being passed out Opperman recognized a young man named Howie Kaibel to speak on behalf of its passage.

Very painful experience has taught me not to rely on first impressions, but within ten seconds I had taken a mild dislike to Howie Kaibel. For one thing, he chose to deliver his remarks while perched on the edge of a table. It was only meant to convey a sense of informality, but it irked me just the same. I remember those table-sitters from my undergraduate days; I was always hoping they'd fall off. What really irritated me, though, was Kaibel's opening line: "Those of us here with a moral point of view already know how we're going to vote on this resolution." The rest of his remarks were delivered with what was—granted his first premise—appropriate contempt for the immoralists in the audience, a group that now included me, it seems, since, moral or not, I was disinclined to vote for any resolution until I'd read it first. This I quickly tried to do, but the document was several pages in length, single-spaced. I skimmed them as hurriedly as possible. Most of the articles were variants on the theme of American perfidy in Vietnam, and to the substance of these I took no real exception. But several others wandered far afield, as when condemning the then proposed federal income tax surcharge for being "undemocratic." The final clause was the one which stopped me, though. It endorsed the McCarthy candidacy for President. This was November 1967, of course, and I wasn't certain at that time whether there *was* a McCarthy candidacy. If so, then it's a pretty safe guess that this resolution was the first political test of it anywhere. And I opposed it. At least, I opposed equating opposition to the war with automatic support of McCarthy for President. I even got up and spoke to this point.

The looks I'd received on arriving were kindly compared to what happened now, when I actually faced the audience with my suggestion that we vote first on Vietnam and then on McCarthy. They weren't buying it. With them, it was a package deal. Accordingly, since at that time I wasn't sure whether even *McCarthy* was supporting McCarthy, I had to vote against the resolution. Despite my opposition, it did sneak through by a two-to-one margin. (The reason I could vote at all is that my far-sighted, near-sighted brother had been prescient enough, after paying the one dollar dues at his first ward club meeting one month earlier, to remove his glasses and, thus disguised as me, to get in line again and sign me up too as a qualified member.) No sooner was the resolution passed when that tireless masochist, Bill Mullin, jumped up to move that we all go on record as commending the efforts toward peace of our great Vice-President, Hubert Humphrey. Bill's desperate appeal to local pride not only failed, but suggested a strong opening line to the reporter from the Minneapolis *Star* who had been seated in the back throughout the meeting. Humphrey's defeat on his home ground would be duly heralded the following day with the front-page headline: DFL WARD CLUB SNUBS HHH. I didn't know it then, but this was only the start of local press aggrandizement of the Sixth Ward Club and its significance in the scheme of things, a process essentially so solipsistic that before long ... well, I'm getting ahead of my story.

After the Mullin motion had been beaten, there was no business left, but before adjournment Vance Opperman talked a bit about "The Canvass." The words were spoken almost reverently. Every resident of the Sixth Ward was to be canvassed before the precinct caucuses that coming March. The canvass would produce all sorts of information about those residents—name, age, address, voting eligibility, party preference —and this information would be fed into a computer. The results would be miraculous. Two-thirds of the Sixth Ward residents, we were told, were basically DFLers. The problem was that they didn't vote. And it was hard to change their apathy because no one really knew who or where they were. That's why the ward's alderman, Jens Christensen, could get away with being a Republican. But the computer would take care of that and in addition would enable the new ward club leadership to turn out unprecedented throngs to the upcoming precinct caucuses. That was the real goal, of course. "Remember the caucuses!" was Opperman's closing admonition. And, "We're going to get Jens."

I had come to the meeting intending to work at the local level. So immediately following adjournment I went up to the front to sign on as a canvasser. As I was adding my name to the surprisingly short list of volunteers, I felt a hand gripping my shoulder. It was Opperman, all smiles, who wanted to welcome me to the ward club. He couldn't have been more amiable. To my amazement, he reeled off all sorts of information about my own past political activity and contacts. He named a number of people whom he was sure we both knew in common. He told me several times how important it was for all of us to work together. With understanding eyebrows he motioned toward his fellow students, some of whom, he had to admit, were a little worked up right now.

"But I'm in for the long haul," he said. "We're going to get Jens."

Thus assured, I left the meeting. And then began one of the most frustrating periods of my life. It seems ridiculous as I look back on it. But no one wants to be excluded from anything, and I suppose this simple fact explains more than anything else my efforts at involvement in the ward club. Beginning with the canvass.

I had left my first ward club meeting fully expecting to be called within a few days at most to help take part in the canvass. The activity itself had no appeal—I'd canvassed once before, in my old ward, and had found it tedious—but I did welcome the chance to meet the student activists in this new club. Despite Opperman's cozy greeting, it still bothered me that I was regarded as an outsider. I wanted to show, in Opperman's constant phrase, that all of us could work together.

As the weeks went on, however, I was never notified of any canvass work and so assumed that the project had been postponed. It hadn't occurred to me that my help might not be wanted. Opperman had been so conciliatory, and not only to me. Shortly after the ward club meeting, he had published in the Minneapolis *Star* a letter attempting to correct its reporter's impression that the club's rejection of Bill Mullin's resolution could in any way be considered a rebuke to Hubert Humphrey. "It would be a disservice to this great man," Opperman's letter read, "to blame him for a policy which he had little responsibility in formulating. I find it hard to believe that if Humphrey had been responsible for this policy that the United States would be in the mess it now is.... We can understand the political necessity of Humphrey's support of Mr. Johnson's policy, but it is totally unfair to criticize Humphrey for the initiation of that policy. It is a disservice to Humphrey's humanitarianism and political creativity." These words certainly suggested that student anti-war sentiment was not going to be permitted to infringe on party harmony. Or party flattery, either.

One night, though, I stopped to get some pizza after a movie, and my waitress turned out to be Katy, the young girl who had been so friendly at the ward club meeting. She still was friendly. She told me that she and Joel had been out ringing doorbells as part of the canvass. I asked her why I hadn't been called to help out, too. She looked embarrassed. Obviously trying very hard not to hurt my feelings, Katy explained the way it was. My association with Bill Mullin, the fact that I'd worked for Mondale, plus my supposed acquaintanceship with other party leaders, had branded me as irretrievably Establishment. My little speech on the Vietnam resolution hadn't helped matters either. Katy claimed that she'd put in some good words for me, but that to the others I remained a very suspicious character.

This was my first glimpse of the students' political paranoia, and I found it irksome that their conjectures were so ill founded. I did know casually a number of state party officers and officeholders, but my experience in city politics was markedly more limited than that of several of those students who had been trying to take over the Sixth Ward Club for three or four years. I was aware that there were two rival factions in Minneapolis DFL politics—organized labor versus a group inexplicably labeled in the press as "the intellectuals"—and that I belonged to neither. I was hoping that the students didn't either and that we shared a common ground.

Whatever the students thought, though, about politics in general or my own tainted past, I was determined to take part in their canvass. I went to the next ward club meeting —almost none of the older members were present this time— and waited for it to end so that I could ask both Opperman and Howie Kaibel why I hadn't been called. The first of these gentlemen was cordial, the other cool, and both unmistakably evasive. But by now my irritation had been supplanted by resolve. And channeled into persistence: during the next week I made such a pest of myself that my demands for inclusion could no longer be ignored. Opperman's phone line was always busy, but at our last meeting, as a gesture of amity, he had given me his unlisted number, or as he called it, "the hot line." So, I could get to him quite frequently, which I did, with tenacity. I phoned so many times to ask when the next canvass was taking place that finally Opperman gave me his word that I'd be included in the very next effort, though he never let himself be pinned down as to when exactly that might be. Kaibel's approach was different. He was always most precise. Every time I called him (he had only one phone), I was asked in terms of pained regret why I hadn't called only the day before, I'd just missed a canvassing operation.

So I started phoning every day.

As a result of all this bother, one Saturday morning *I* got a call from Kaibel. He said that if I wanted to help, I could —they were all setting out from Opperman's house in fifteen minutes.

My first reaction is unprintable, and I barely managed not to share it with Kaibel. I was in my pajamas, unshaven, not really awake yet. Through my bedroom window I could see that the recent snow had already become a grayish sludge. It was undoubtedly very cold out there. My apartment was

13

comfortable and warm. And fifteen minutes is not a lot of notice. But Kaibel surely knew this too—he was, in fact, probably counting on it—so I agreed to come right over. I was even able to sound enthusiastic. Ten minutes later I was on my way, wondering what I was trying to prove and praying that there'd be some fresh coffee at Opperman's.

2

I'd never really been on the West Bank before, at least not since the student migration there, and I had trouble finding Opperman's house. The narrow streets were contracted still further by unremoved snow and stalled cars. I had trouble seeing the numbers on the houses as I slowly maneuvered my car around potholes and impacted snow. The houses were old and dingy. The only new buildings were several small apartment houses, stark and ugly, with an unfinished look about them.

I finally found Opperman's house, but the closest parking spot was a block away. The sidewalks were unshoveled and I had to walk along the single narrow lane which had been cleared in the middle of the street. In my haste I had forgotten to put on boots, and, as my shoes got progressively soggier, I came to understand how very appealing was Opperman's promise to replace the incumbent alderman with someone who at least could attend to snow removal.

The house, like many others in the area, had been converted into a duplex, and the Oppermans lived on the first floor. I entered through an open wooden corridor which once had been part of the porch. The first thing I noticed was Howie Kaibel's face, and his unmistakable surprise that I'd been able to get there in the time prescribed almost made up for the three large puddles which I'd recently failed to traverse.

Opperman's wife, Sue, very cool and attractive, came to get my coat and then led me further into the living room. There were twelve or fifteen others present, of whom Opperman, at twenty-four, was probably the oldest, not counting me. And most of them *weren't* counting me. At my arrival, conversation came to a stop and was not resumed after the introductions had been completed. The only sound in the room was my squeaking shoes as I searched in vain for an empty chair. Sue steered me to a hassock and then brought me a cup of coffee, which I very badly needed. After awhile some quiet conversations started up again, but I was not included. So I sipped my coffee and looked around the room.

On more than one occasion, when I had called and asked Vance Opperman questions about the canvass, he had tried to change the subject by talking about himself. His house confirmed much of what he'd said. It was somewhat more comfortable than most student housing. This was probably due to his wife's taste, I thought, but a number of items in the book-lined rooms suggested a relative freedom of expenditure, too. I knew that Vance's father, a former F.B.I. man, was now the President of West Publishing Company and that he helped his son out with a monthly stipend, "a scholarship from home," Vance called it. This accounted, no doubt, for the unlisted phone number and a rather extensive set of aquariums, one of which contained a very small shark.

My perusal of the walls was interrupted by the forceful voice of our host, who was beginning an instructive little talk about the canvass. He had a number of maps and said that each of us would be assigned in teams of two to cover an area four blocks square. We were to go up to each doorbell, ring it, inform the occupant that we were with the DFL party and wished to ask a few questions. These included the names, ages, and marital status of the occupants. And, most important, their party affiliation. If they said they were DFLers, we were to ask them to come to their precinct caucus on March 5.

But that wasn't all. Opperman paused a minute, looked at me, and seemed reluctant to continue. He must have felt he had no choice but to go on, for finally he announced that there was another question, too. Each canvasser should ask the occupant what he thought about the war. If anyone was against it, he was to be urged not only to come to the caucus, but to vote for the McCarthy slate as well.

So that's why I hadn't been wanted. When ward club members conduct a canvass, they are not supposed to push for one faction or another. They are just supposed to turn out as many members of their party as possible. This group was actively recruiting for McCarthy and didn't want me to know it.

I was genuinely touched by their discomfort. I was impressed that they didn't know what even I was aware of: that factional canvassing, though incorrect in principle, was very widely practiced everywhere in the city. In fact it was the norm. The rationale was that anyone willing to go out and ring doorbells was entitled to push his own candidates. To do so under the color of regular party effort wasn't quite fair, but it had ample precedent. I was amused that they thought I'd object. In their inexperience they'd evidently imagined that some dire penalty would attach to their work for McCarthy. All that concern over something which was very common practice, and impossible to monitor in any case. My own reaction was, if anything, favorable. Politics needs a little more naïveté.

And of course I'd known all along what they were doing. I'd just *assumed* it. Several of the students in Opperman's living room, waiting now for my reaction, were wearing McCarthy buttons. (Not the blue and green one, that hadn't appeared yet. Some of the students had found buttons from McCarthy's last Senate campaign, four years before.) Their allegiance was so public, why should I be surprised if they sought to promote it? I asked if it would be all right if I didn't question people as to whether they were supporting McCarthy and confined myself to the other questions. Opperman solemnly said that would be fine. Everyone looked relieved.

That hurdle crossed, Opperman began to give out the street assignments. As there was an even number of volunteers present, I had to be assigned to someone and was paired up with a young graduate student in sociology who had been the last to arrive. We were equipped with index cards and pencils and then driven to our area about a mile away.

The work was depressing. The neighborhood was terribly run-down. It was surprising how many people were not at home or, at least, did not come to their doors. Many of the doorbells were out of order, and we had to pound away on the front door to get anyone's attention. I had been told that this was a student area, but it certainly didn't seem that way. Most of the people I talked to were old, retired and very poor. Some of them didn't have telephones. By far the most destitute were the Indians. In my one previous canvassing experience, in my old ward, I had spent most of my time in Minneapolis' largest ghetto area and had seen firsthand that most of the blacks there were disadvantaged. But that was middle-class compared to this.

The level of political interest was discouragingly low. A typical encounter went like this:

ME: Hello, I'm with the DFL party, and I'd like to take just a minute to ask a few questions.
THEY: What for?
ME: Well, we're just taking a little survey. May I ask your name, sir?
THEY: (Somewhat defensively giving name.)
ME: Is that Jenson with an "e" or with an "o"?
THEY: "O."
ME: And may I ask if you're registered to vote?
THEY: You bet.
ME: Fine. Did you vote in the last election?
THEY: I think so. Which one was that?
ME: Rolvaag. For Governor.
THEY: I think I did.
ME: And may I ask what party you belong to?
THEY: Well, I don't know. Who did you say you were with?
ME: The Democratic-Farmer-Labor party.

THEY: Oh sure. The Farmer-Labor. I guess that's what I am.

ME: Well, we certainly hope you'll come to our precinct caucus on March 5.

THEY: What's there?

ME: We'll be sending you a notice, of course, to remind you, but that's the night when everyone gets together and votes for delegates from your precinct. And then those delegates go on and vote for other delegates. They're the ones who finally get to choose who the delegates will be to the Democratic National Convention.

THEY: (Prolonged silence.)

ME: In Chicago.

THEY: (More silence.)

ME: You see, if there's any subject you feel strongly about, you can vote for people who agree with you. Like on the war.

THEY: The war? I don't know.

ME: Or our alderman. You know, we've got to beat this Republican alderman.

THEY: Jens? I thought he was Farmer-Labor.

ME: Oh, no. He's a Republican. His *uncle*, who used to be your alderman, was a DFLer. But Jens is a Republican.

THEY: Well, he ought to get this goddam snow off the streets.

ME: I agree. If you want to do something about it, come out to our caucus on March 5.

THEY: How does that get rid of the snow?

ME: Well, you see, you vote for delegates and for party officers, and they can endorse someone good to run against our Republican alderman.

THEY: Does this cost anything?

ME: No, it's free. All you do is come and vote.

THEY: Jens did put in a street light. Are you sure he ain't Farmer-Labor?

ME: Positive. Absolutely.

THEY: Well, that's something. I tell you what, I'll think about it.
ME: Thanks very much. We'll send you a reminder. And may I just ask, sir, if there are any other adult members of your household?
THEY: The wife, but she's sick.
ME: Oh, I'm sorry. And do you have a phone?
THEY: Yes.
ME: I wonder if I can have your number?
THEY: Well, I don't know.
ME: That's all right. I just hope we'll be seeing you March 5.
THEY: Yeah. OK. So long.

Of course, it didn't always go that way. Some of the residents were very well informed. They had been to previous caucuses and said they were grateful to be notified about the next one. Many of the student residents had heard about the caucus and were already planning to attend. In these instances it was mostly a question of reminding them to register; only registered voters could take part in a caucus. The students who planned to attend were in almost every case motivated solely by their opposition to the war, whereas the other residents had more immediate concerns. It was surprising how many agreed to come simply on learning that their alderman was a Republican. It wasn't that they were for the war, most of them were against it; but they balked at the idea of voting against an incumbent President of their own party.

By mid-afternoon I was feeling pretty good. For one thing, my teammate, the graduate student, was now considerably friendlier. We had been working opposite sides of the street, but he had been nearby and overheard me urging a girl, a Republican she said, to attend our caucus even after she'd told me that she intended to vote for McCarthy. So if I wasn't a part of their faction, at least he knew I wasn't subverting it.

And I felt that I was getting something done. Despite some occasional rudeness and a lot of people not being home, I had managed to fill out quite a few index cards. The information on each was sketchy, but I could see how it would help. If these few blocks were at all typical, then Opperman was right in assuming that most Sixth Ward residents were DFLers. It was very clear that if we were able to get their names and addresses and phone numbers, we would indeed be able to turn out record numbers to the caucuses. And of course using a computer for this kind of work would make it that much easier. It was such a natural way to proceed, I wondered why no one had done this sort of work in other years. In just one afternoon I had managed to cover several square blocks. The graduate student in sociology was moving somewhat more slowly, since he often stopped to argue with those who disagreed with him on the war. I didn't spend much time on that and concentrated on getting as many names as possible. By dusk the two of us had over one hundred.

We were just debating whether or not to branch out into unassigned territory when a car pulled up to take us back to Opperman's. This time I was much more welcome. Everyone seemed to share a sense of accomplishment. Howie Kaibel carried out a case of beer from Opperman's kitchen, and we relaxed a little as we waited for the stragglers to return. We sat around and swapped stories about how it had gone. One fellow had been threatened, another propositioned, and a third had been bitten by a dog. He looked very proud about it and kept insisting that his wound was slight.

Opperman was busy with his master map of the Sixth Ward. After collating all the cards, he shaded in with ink the area just canvassed, and though this dark blue spot seemed unwarrantably small, covering not even one precinct, the sight of it enhanced the happy spirit of the workers. Opperman took advantage of the mood to remind everyone of the work yet to be done. He explained that in addition to the canvass, there was the job of feeding the new data into a computer. Several people volunteered for this, including, I'm afraid, myself, still glowing from my new acceptability, and others promised to come back the next week and ring doorbells.

It was then I learned that Opperman's organization was not confined to one ward. He was asking for volunteers to canvass the Ninth Ward, and the Second. Both these areas had large student populations, but I was surprised to learn that Opperman's plans were so extensive. It seemed to me difficult enough to cover even one ward. But the response from the students was favorable. Several promised to bring friends the next time.

As if to spur their efforts, someone repeated a rumor that organized labor was starting a Sixth Ward canvass of its own. This news was received with anguished groans. The students simply *assumed* that the unions were their enemy and a dangerous one at that, resourceful and ruthless. My own views as to organized labor's motives and efficiency were very different. Surely if there had been a rival labor effort we would have heard about it during our own canvass. But no resident had indicated to me that anyone else had been there before. Yet the very prospect of such action seemed real enough to anger and frighten the students. I was certain they were wrong: they seemed to feel so strongly that unseen and powerful forces were opposing them. The State Central Committee of the DFL had just changed some procedural rules affecting the caucus, and this, too, was thought to be part of a dark, coordinated plot. The boy who'd been bitten by the dog spoke excitedly about his concern, and the others seemed to look on him as a kind of symbolic victim for the rest. I attributed their reaction to simple inexperience and was reasonably sure that they'd get over it soon.

It was well past dinnertime and I was starting out the door with the others when Opperman drew me aside and asked if I'd stay behind for a few minutes. He said he had something to discuss. So I stood around and studied the small shark for some minutes while the students said their good-byes and finally left. On a table by the aquarium there was a copy of the latest S.D.S. *Newsletter*. I'd never seen one before. I had heard that Opperman was the past Chairman of the Minnesota S.D.S. chapter, although from his recent activities I had come to assume that he now preferred less insurgent paths to political participation. He certainly didn't talk like a radical, at least not to me. I remembered his letter to the editor praising Hubert Humphrey—I couldn't figure him out. His wife, too, seemed so quiet and gentle, and yet I knew that she was very active in a militant Arab group at the University, fanatically anti-Israel.

Vance came back into the room. He told me how much he'd been looking forward to having a little chat with me. As he went on though, the little chat turned out to be merely a repetition of his public remarks on the desirability of all of us working together. That was a supposition I'd never denied. I didn't need convincing. But he continued at some length about how wonderful it would be to have students and labor and everyone else all pulling together.

"You know," he related, "we're going to come out of this with a new party, and I'd like to see to it that you're a part of it."

I thanked him for the sentiment, but said I thought that everyone was going to be part of it. He smiled.

"You know what I'm trying to say," he confided. But I didn't.

I had plans for the evening and was already late, so I got up and started looking for my coat. At the door, I turned and made a little joke about what his new broad coalition would think of the S.D.S. *Newsletter.*

Opperman sprang into action. He dashed across the room and hurried back with the newsletter. He was pointing to its address label.

"This isn't mine," he said. "This isn't mine. My wife subscribes, but I don't any more. See, here's Sue's name, right here."

Sue looked at Vance but said nothing. I thanked him for the beer and left.

Throughout January of 1968 I was very busy with my work, but I remained fairly active in the ward club. I really had no choice. Having achieved some measure of acceptance, I was now the object, not the source, of frantic phone calls. There were never enough volunteers it seems, so I tried to help out when I could. I'd made a number of new friends among the students and saw quite a few of them socially. They were good company, except perhaps for their habit of phoning at two in the morning (their own day began around noon) and an almost total conversational preoccupation with local politics. They were obsessed with political organization. If I asked where so-and-so lived, I'd be told that she had an apartment in the Seventeenth Precinct. I knew several of the DFL state officers, middle-aged and somewhat skeptical of West Bank activists, and I kept wishing that they could meet these students. And vice versa. If only my new young friends knew how hard their older counterparts in the party had been trying, or for how long, to bring about some grass-roots organization. Both groups should have been working together. I continued to be amazed, though, at how suspicious the students were of the regular party members. In fact, I didn't see why they even called them that; no activity could have been more "regular" than the incessant canvassing efforts of the students themselves.

Of course, I didn't agree with everything they did. I was troubled, for example, that one of the first actions of the new ward leadership was to remove effectively most of the club decision-making powers from the membership and place it instead with a small Central Committee composed of those close to Opperman and Kaibel. This made it virtually impossible for anyone else to take over the ward club at a regular meeting, as they themselves had done. I was disappointed that so few students opposed this move. Its most outspoken opponent, to my surprise, was the fellow named Jock, whose remarkable head of hair and fiercely drooping moustache I still remembered from my first ward club meeting. (His appearance was so spectacular that they only let him canvass certain precincts.) But his appeal for consistency did no good. The Ward Central Committee was established.

And the students were so terribly suspicious. I think I used the word "paranoid" earlier, and it's really not unfair. One fellow, for example, a law student, felt emboldened enough one evening after we'd had a few drinks together to actually ask me if the rumor was true that Senator Mondale was paying my rent.

"My *what?*" I asked.

"The rent on your apartment. I mean, some of us kind of thought that's the reason you moved back from Washington.

We thought maybe he set you up here to sort of, you know, keep him informed about what's going on in the club."

What could I say? What could they possibly be thinking about the way things happen in this world or about my own character for that matter, not to mention Mondale's financial resources. However bizarre it was, though, the view was very commonly shared.

And I doubted whether a more relaxed approach was very likely, at least in the near future. There was clearly an increase in tension within the DFL. The McCarthy candidacy was by now a fact, and some people were already talking about a split in the party. In December my sister Judy had gone with friends to attend something called the Conference of Concerned Democrats in Chicago. Having heard Senator McCarthy state officially that he was in the race for President, she had returned full of determination to support him. We argued about it all the time. I agreed with her about the war, and she agreed with me that McCarthy had no chance of being nominated, but from there we parted company—rather angrily, I regret to say, on more than one occasion. She discussed my opinion with a mutual friend who worked for *Newsweek*, and he wrote me a three-page letter in which my own views, somewhat distorted, were frequently analogized with those of the German populace in 1939. It was the first time I'd been called a Fascist and by a friend whose intellect I very much respected too; but, of course, at that point I had no idea of what the coming months would be like.

The simple fact is that I was able to distinguish between unacceptance of the McCarthy candidacy and my opposition to the war. That's why I continued to support the Sixth Ward students, though I'd made it very clear to them that I wasn't going to back their candidate at the caucus. I didn't believe that an incumbent President could be denied renomination by his own party. I understood that such an effort of itself might help to change the Administration's approach to the war, but the price of that persuasion seemed to me to risk divisiveness to such a degree that the election itelf would be in doubt. I was pretty sure that Richard Nixon would be the Republican candidate, and I didn't want to see him win. So I intended at the caucus to vote for the slate of delegates loyal to the Administration. But at the same caucus we would elect ward officers for the next two years, and there I had no trouble at all in strongly backing the students. No matter how the vote on delegates went, there was no question but that the young new activists had instilled much energy and purpose into what had been a moribund club. I guess what I believed in most of all was the extension of political participation at the grass-roots level. The students were surely doing that, bringing hundreds of new people into the party. At the very least, they ought to be allowed to retain control of the organization which they'd so painstakingly revitalized. They had made it very clear that they wanted to work closely with all the other factions in the party, and I felt good about backing them for the officer posts.

I was particularly glad when it came time to work on the computer project. This was to be the culmination of all our other efforts. We'd been hearing about the computer for months; Opperman never missed a chance to mention it. All the work, all the time, all the patient door-to-door canvassing, had been to gather data to be programmed and now was the time to start.

I showed up, as requested, at Howie Kaibel's apartment early on a Sunday evening in January. A group had been out all day ringing doorbells and since some of them were going to work on the computer program, too, we had to wait for their return before we could set out for the data-processing plant. My first impression of Kaibel had softened somewhat as we worked together, though he continued to regard me with considerable suspicion. Tonight, however, he was all smiles, almost euphoric, and very anxious to get going. The computer was his special project. His father was a manager at the data-processing plant, so Howie had been able to make all the arrangements for our evening's furtive use of the equipment. If to Opperman the computer was invaluable, to Kaibel its significance was close to magic. When the canvassers came in, he didn't even let them take their boots off. We all left right away to work on the computer.

What we actually worked on was punch cards. The place that Howie's father managed was at the end of a long dark street of buildings and was itself pitch dark when we arrived. But Mr. Kaibel was there as scheduled and led us through several dim and empty offices to a large and very brightly lighted workroom in the back. All around were strange machines of varying size, each sufficiently formidable. These, it was explained, could not be used until we'd done our work, which turned out to be the punch cards.

Mr. Kaibel described very carefully what it was we were to do. Each card, the standard rectangular IBM variety, was to be fitted into a small machine. Using a keyboard, we were to punch upon the card the name and address of a canvassed resident and symbols for other information, such as age, sex, voter registration status, precinct. Once that was done, we inserted another card and started again with the next name.

My own mechanical aptitude can best be judged by the costly fact that I still can't change a tire. I listened to the instructions with great apprehension. The others didn't seem to be comprehending things any better than I. And there weren't very many of us, anyway. Seven or eight, as I recall, and not standard key-punch operators either. There were two girls who shared an apartment which had been canvassed just that afternoon; they were new in town and wanted to meet some new people so they had come along to help out for an evening. Then Opperman, Kaibel, and a few others. Katy's husband, Joel, an engineering student, and Howie Kaibel presumably had programmed cards before; the rest of us were very nervous.

For several hours we worked at our key punches. The first few cards were a disaster. Even when we got them right-side-up (in my own case that took until the fourth try), it seemed awfully easy to hit the wrong keys. Howie's father kept coming around and checking up on us—I'll say this, he never lost his temper. He'd just explain very carefully what had gone wrong and after awhile we seemed to get the hang of it. My pile of finished cards grew reassuringly high. By eleven o'clock I'd programmed several precincts. It was pleasant to come across a name I'd actually canvassed myself and surprising how frequently that occurred.

We didn't stop until we were completely out of names. Then we took the cards with their hopefully meaningful punctures and put them all in a single pile. There weren't as many as I thought. We were told not to worry about sorting them—the computer would do that.

Then Howie's father led everyone into the next room, which was full of large, interconnected machines so we could see a sample of how the whole thing worked. He took a finished card at random from one of the girls and fed it into the apparatus. A humming and whirring began at once, and a sharp little clicking started in across the room. The group was quiet, watching. They seemed awed that one little card could produce such a cacophonous reaction, and equally impressed that all this equipment was somehow on their side. It was a reversal of the student role, this hope and trust they put in an IBM card.

The machine suddenly stopped, and a neatly printed page slid down a chute. "Now here," Mr. Kaibel explained, "is all the dope on someone in your ward." Everyone crowded around to see it and then stopped in amazement. The individual so permanently defined on the emergent sheet was none other than Jock, their hirsute co-worker. They seemed stunned at the thought of any relationship between a friend—someone they *knew*, so unconventional that he had to be kept under wraps during the canvass—and the neat political summary sheet that they had themselves produced this evening.

They were jubilant. Humor is not the long suit of these student political activists, but they were joking now, relaxed and happy and very clearly proud of what they had accomplished. But I wasn't entirely sure. I had been hearing for so long about the computer and what it could do. It was supposed to make everything possible: endless mailing lists, the recruitment of campaign workers, solicitation of funds. Looking around, I somehow felt a sense of disappointment. There should have been more workers. We hadn't really done that many cards. The caucus was less than two months away. I dismissed these thoughts as unworthy. Perhaps this evening's work had not been typical. Surely Opperman and Kaibel and the others would see to it that all the hours of work of all their friends would be employed in some effective way. I found myself hoping so.

3

When in political doubt I often call a friend who, pseudonymously, I shall refer to as the Doctor's Wife. She's a very fine person. Intelligent, decent, principled. I like her husband, too. They have a splendid family. Their children are precocious and delightful. They all live in a very large house with a wide and unobstructed view of one of our city's most scenic lakes. They read a lot and have collected a number of pretty good paintings. Some evenings they host chamber music concerts in their home and these occasions never fail to be rewarding.

The Doctor's Wife is fairly active in Minneapolis city politics. To be precise, she spends a great deal of time helping the campaigns of our Congressman, Donald Fraser, a remarkable man of whom we're both fanatical supporters. In fact, Congressman Fraser is our common political bond. We disagree about most other things. When we get off the subject of Fraser, we invariably end up in political disaccord—and always over tactics, never goals. The Doctor's Wife is not concerned with tactics; her approach to things political is breathtakingly direct. She thinks very carefully about what is right and then proceeds toward it in a straight unswerving line of quiet rectitude. Very few of her political causes have ever been successful. I'm always chiding her to be more realistic, though I must admit a grudging sort of awe for her absolute unwillingness to contemplate even the possibility of compromise.

In politics, her favorite word is "moral." Well, that's not

quite right—the word "immoral" is what she seems to use most often in trying to make a point. Conduct or theory with which she disagrees is very apt to be immoral. People, too. With her the word is not susceptible to even mild refinement by degree.

But she tries very hard to be fair. And as I've said, she's exceedingly bright. It's worth all the arguments with which our conversations are so apt to end because later, more reflectively, and quite often against my will, I tend to find my views improved (that's just the kind of word she would use) by the painful intrusion of some insight which I simply can't deny. That's why I call her when I think perhaps I ought to hear another point of view.

The Doctor's Wife was a very strong McCarthy supporter. And so, excepting me, were all her friends. (All her friends always share identical views on any political matter.) Yet at this stage we still had considerable basis for agreement. She approved very strongly of my helping out the West Bank students and was eager to learn more about them—although, I was surprised to learn, she'd already had a call from Opperman, who wanted her help in the campaign.

The reason that I wanted her advice was that things were getting out of hand in local politics. The mood was very ugly. By late February few DFLers even talked about avoiding a party split. The split was there. And very public, too. Two high-ranking state party officers, the First Vice-Chairman and Vice-Chairwoman, had come out openly for McCarthy. I wasn't too surprised about the First Vice-Chairwoman. She's the kind of Democrat who thinks John Lindsay has something new to say. But the decision of the First Vice-Chairman, Forrest Harris, made a great impression on me. Harris is a Professor at the University of Minnesota, a long-time party activist, a very decent man, and he had more cause than anyone else I knew to despise McCarthy thoroughly. Years before, a personal crisis had forced him to look for a job that paid more than the one he had at the University. With what must have been real despondency, he had gone to his friend Congressman Fraser and asked his help in being named to the vacant postmastership of Minneapolis. It's a standard custom of congressional privilege to permit a congressman to choose the postmaster of his own home town, which in Fraser's case is Minneapolis. Fraser submitted Harris' name. I'm sure everyone involved felt that confirmation would be automatic. And it would have been, too, except that Forrest Harris had once somehow offended Gene McCarthy. I'm sure he hadn't meant to. The way I'd heard it, Harris, as a member of the DFL State Executive Committee, had joined in signing a letter to McCarthy in which the Senator was asked why he was supporting some qualifications to the 1964 Civil Rights Act. McCarthy apparently resented either the tone or the fact of such questioning of his behavior, and he proved to have quite a memory. So when he heard, years later, that Harris had been nominated by Fraser, he went to the trouble of contacting his then friend, President Johnson, and asked that another man be given the job. He didn't bother to tell Harris about this or Fraser either, for that matter. They both found out about it by reading in the paper that the McCarthy-Johnson man had been named Postmaster. Harris never talked about this, but he must have been terribly hurt. So when he came out publicly for Gene McCarthy, I had to admire the extent of his opposition to the war. He was certainly putting principle above a legitimate personal grudge.

Many other DFLers, less prominent in the party, were voicing their support of the McCarthy candidacy, too. It wasn't just the students, though they were getting almost all of the attention. The press had heard of the Sixth Ward effort, and Opperman and Kaibel were becoming quite well known in political circles. They'd opened up a small office on the West Bank, and this headquarters seemed to serve as a focus for publicity. The brave student challenge of a huge and powerful organization makes a very appealing story. But, no matter who was responsible for it, or to what extent, the McCarthy movement was very clearly gaining steam.

More to the point, it was gaining delegates. On March 5 the precinct caucuses would be held. Minnesota has almost four thousand precincts. Each precinct caucus elects delegates to the county convention on the same night that the city elects delegates to the ward convention. Each ward convention then elects delegates to the state convention. The Sixth Ward, for example, would elect seven state delegates. Seven out of over twelve hundred. Of course, many other wards had McCarthy supporters, too, although no one thought it even remotely possible that there were enough of them to win enough wards and counties in order to control the state convention.

But they might take over a congressional district. That was possible. The Fifth Congressional District—that's Don Fraser's—encompasses the city of Minneapolis. The city has thirteen wards, and the state convention delegates from those wards make up the Fifth District Convention. It was just conceivable that a majority of the ward delegates to the Fifth District Convention would elect five delegates to the Democratic National Convention in Chicago. So would each of the other seven district conventions, making forty delegates to Chicago. The state convention would select twenty more, at-large.

It was the Fifth District that the Administration forces were worried about. All the publicity that Opperman was getting had made them nervous. There were even some alarmists who were pointing to McCarthy organizations in the suburbs and St. Paul—the Third and Fourth Congressional Districts—but the McCarthy prospects there were dim at best. Unlike Minneapolis, there were no highly visible student leaders in either the Third or the Fourth, and no computer either.

The Fifth District was the real concern. The DFL State Chairman, Warren Spannaus, had spread that concern while trying to contain it. Returning from a tour of northwestern Minnesota, Spannaus had been quoted by the Minneapolis *Star* as predicting that Senator McCarthy "won't get more than six national convention delegates from Minnesota." No more than six meant six were possible. There was no question as to where they might come from. The Fifth District could actually be taken by McCarthy. That would be five delegates. And naturally Minnesota's senior Senator would be permitted, as a courtesy, to be one of the twenty at-large envoys to Chicago. That would be six delegates. The Administration forces hur-

31

riedly redoubled their own efforts to get ready for the caucuses. A large Johnson-Humphrey headquarters had been opened in downtown Minneapolis.

Feeling was running very high. If awareness of a threat had mobilized defenders of the Administration ticket, then the Tet offensive in Vietnam, with all its harsh but undeniable truth, had caused the ranks of the McCarthy cause to swell. Each side grew more distrustful of the other as the day set for the caucuses came closer into view. The anxiety of the students now surpassed by far even the suspiciousness which they had felt before. Opperman fed their fears by reporting that he had been offered a sizable bribe in exchange for a few Sixth Ward delegates. Was there no limit to the duplicity of the foe? One young man volunteered to stay on guard duty every night with a loaded shotgun in the Sixth Ward headquarters in order to repel the attack which so many thought inevitable.

I knew these fears to be unfounded. The Minnesota Chairman of the Johnson-Humphrey effort, state Senator Wendell Anderson, was a close friend of mine. Tough but fair, he would have been astounded had he heard those tales of plots which the students took as gospel. For the truth is that despite Anderson's own hard work and first-rate mind, the Administration forces were having serious trouble in even getting off the ground. The party rank-and-file were apathetic. They would not, for the most part, support McCarthy, but neither were they anxious to bestir themselves for Lyndon Johnson. Organized labor supplied lists of party faithful to be called to attend the caucuses, but there were not enough volunteers to do the calling. Retired people, elderly ladies, had to be hired by the hour to do the job.

And everywhere that DFLers came together socially the signs of open acrimony were impossible to avoid. Every meeting or party seemed to end in an argument. The DFL officeholders were under pressure from both sides. I was trying to raise money for Don Fraser, whose Republican opponent was the most formidable in years and quite well financed; every time I asked a labor leader for some help, I had to try to explain why Fraser wasn't more outspoken in his support of the

Administration. In soliciting the McCarthy supporters, it was the other way around: how *could* Don have come out at all for those Fascist warmongers, especially in light of his own early and unqualified opposition to the war? Everyone had some complaint, no one could be mollified.

That's why I called the Doctor's Wife. Her dedication to Fraser was unbounded. I wanted us to find some way of opposing the war without splitting the party. But I had trouble reaching her. She was conscientiously trying to phone every possible McCarthy ally in her own ward, and it took several days before I was able to get through.

I should have saved my time. We covered all the pros and cons and ended up precisely where we always had before. There was simply no room to maneuver. I told the Doctor's Wife that if things continued in this way, the local candidates for office would have to offend one faction or the other. She said they should all come out for McCarthy. I said that there must be some other way to show our opposition to the war. She said there was no other way. I said I didn't want to lose the coming fall election. She said that my thinking was immoral.

Perhaps it was, though I didn't think so then and still don't now. I was angry without focus. I couldn't understand why people who desired the same public good should have to oppose one another in order to obtain it. And I didn't think our impasse was a question of morality. A person can be right or wrong without being either moral or immoral. But who was right? And who was wrong?

All the months of patient effort appeared now as a languid prelude to those last few weeks before the caucuses. Both sides really went to work. From Washington, Senator Mondale sent his chief political aide, Michael Berman, to help coordinate the local Johnson-Humphrey drive. I visited the headquarters, large and neat and very orderly, where several dozen ladies were placing phone calls to encourage a full turnout on March 5. I noticed, though, that the lists from which they were calling were in many cases several years old—attendance lists from caucuses in the past. There had been little effort to conduct a fresh canvass, to contact people who had never come out for a caucus before. It would have been hard to do so anyway—there were very few volunteers—but I couldn't help contrasting this last-minute telephone operation with the active and long-term recruitment activities of the students in my ward club.

The contrast was even more vivid when I dropped in at the Sixth Ward office. It was only one long narrow room but it was filled with workers. More workers than phones, in fact, and newly arriving volunteers were being given lists to call from their homes. I expected these lists to be print-outs from our friendly ward computer, and I did see some of these, but many other names were being given out on the same handwritten cards which had been filled out door-to-door. And in still other cases they were using the same old caucus lists upon which the Administration forces were relying. I had presumed that by this time the computer lists would be completed. And they may have been, for all I knew, at least so far as the Sixth Ward was concerned, since this phoning operation was now city-wide in scope and many parts of town had seen no canvassing at all.

Some students were being given lists to call in a labor ward where no chance at all existed for a McCarthy victory. I asked Opperman if this was the best use of his workers' time, and he seemed surprised at the question.

"I know we can't win that ward," he said, "but we can take several precincts."

"What good does it do to win a few precincts if you're going to lose the ward? Why not concentrate on the places where you're strong?"

Opperman thought I was kidding. "There's more than just the *caucuses,* you know. Every precinct has some votes at the county convention, too."

"The county convention?"

He paused for a minute and then apparently decided that the discussion need go no further.

"I think you know what I'm talking about."

Every time he said that, I felt like a fool. I wished he would be less mysterious. I had never been to a county convention but I didn't see how anything it did could affect the McCarthy cause in any way. Hennepin County is so large—covering all of Minneapolis and most of its suburbs—that the party had stopped using it as a vehicle of delegate selection. Instead, state delegates were chosen on the ward level. The Hennepin County convention picked no delegates at all. The county organization was kept in existence partly to comply with state law, though it also served as the focus of local party fundraising, and the last few Hennepin County chairmen, like the incumbent, Bill Mullin, had found their title useful only when issuing public statements. A full-time, paid staff man did most of the actual work.

Opperman shifted the subject to a matter much closer to home. He was now a candidate for party office. The Steering Committee of the ward had recently met and come up with two slates for the caucuses—one for delegates and another for ward club officers. Opperman was named to run for Chairman of the ward club. I thought he already held that post, but he reminded me that he was only filling out an unexpired term. The official election would be at the caucus. If any caucus in the state would be won by the McCarthy faction, it would certainly be in the Sixth Ward. Yet Opperman was very nervous about his chances of winning.

It seems he now had competition. A candidate had emerged to head the Administration slate—Irving Nemerov, a well known lawyer who had been a controversial figure in DFL city politics for many years and was perhaps best known as an intimate of former Governor Rolvaag. But Nemerov had only very recently moved into the ward—into my apartment house in fact, which must have paralyzed that paranoid who still thought Mondale paid my rent. It was hard to see how he could drum up any significant support in the brief time remaining before our caucus.

Still, Opperman was worried. Bill Mullin, whom the students had virtually excluded from ward activity since their take-over months before, told me that Opperman had asked him to place his name in nomination at the caucus. If Opperman was willing to be so publicly identified with an Establishment figure like the Hennepin County Chairman, then he must have thought it possible that the older party regulars would indeed turn out in force.

He even seemed worried about me. At least, that's the impression I got a few days later when he called to chat. He wanted to know if I had any idea of what Nemerov was up to. I told him truthfully that I did not. After we'd gone through this several times he seemed relatively satisfied and launched into a long attack, none too specific, on the boundless perfidy of the Nemerov forces. There was nothing they wouldn't stoop to. I listened to this catalogue of dark intrigue but found it very hard to believe that any group could be that energetic. According to Opperman, Nemerov had troops everywhere in the ward, ready to claim on caucus night that the students were not legal residents of their precincts and could not therefore participate. Opperman had quickly bestirred the students to rush over to City Hall and buy copies of their voter registration certificates in order to meet the rumored challenge. I thought his precautions harmless but unnecessary. However, I was somewhat annoyed by his repeated threat to "fight fire with fire if necessary." And I was becoming tired of having to repeat so many times that, yes, I certainly did intend to back the student slate of officers. I thought I'd made that very clear.

But for some reason Opperman felt that I still needed persuading; not persuading to vote for the McCarthy slate of delegates—from the outset I'd explained why I didn't think I should. All he seemed to care about was the officer slate, and, to bolster my already strong commitment to it, he recited once again his own sublime belief in party unity. If he were chairman he and all his friends would work as never before toward traditional goals—electing aldermen, legislators, and any other DFL-endorsed candidates. They would beat Jens. They would reach out to labor, to the old as well as to the young. There was room for everyone in the DFL.

As if to further gain my confidence, he began to share in great detail the secret plans of the city-wide McCarthy organization. I was shocked at his disclosures, shocked that he would speak so freely to an open if reluctant supporter of the Administration slate. And shocked at how extensive the organization had become. There were organizing efforts other than his own, of course, but he seemed to know everything about them all. I told him that he really ought not to be letting me in on all this, but he insisted on relating the clandestine success of a girl he'd put to work recruiting McCarthy supporters in the Twelfth Ward. Of all places to try to get delegates, I thought. Then I told Opperman a story about the Twelfth Ward that I'd heard from a man who lived there. During a previous party fight he had promised Governor Rolvaag that the Twelfth Ward caucus would deliver at least two hundred votes to him. "There weren't even two hundred people *there*," the man explained, "but you see I'd given my word; so when we counted up our votes I saw to it all right that Rolvaag had his two hundred." The area did not seem promising for opponents of the regular party structure. But Opperman rambled on. He told of efforts in the Fifth Ward, the Eighth, the Thirteenth. In all of these he spoke of specific precincts which his workers would control. He made another of his oblique references to the significance of those precincts at the county convention. I still wasn't sure just what that significance would be, but the scope of the organization seemed impressive.

With each passing day I was happier that soon we'd be through with the caucus. I could hardly wait. I was tired of all the talk and acrimony and suspicion. Once we had those damn caucuses out of the way, though, things were sure to settle back to normal. Better than normal, in fact. The students would win some victories and achieve proper recognition within the party. That would be a good thing. New ideas, new energy. I just wished it would hurry up and happen.

Because those last few days before the caucus were beginning to get on my nerves. The party people and reporters, too, were speculating as to just how well the McCarthy supporters would do. Some claimed that if they were to capture any district, it would most likely be the Fifth. A few said that the

Fourth offered a better chance of victory. Some even suggested the Third. Most thought it would be none at all. Even the students were predicting victories only in specific wards.

But hope springs suspicion, and in at least one case the students' fears were justified. Bill Mullin told me that he had decided not to give the nominating speech for Opperman. He had been visited by what he called the North Siders, whom he described as being less than veiled in itemizing the political consequences to him if he should publicly support the student officer slate. I found this fact intolerable but, knowing the gentlemen involved, was inclined to believe that it had really happened.

And somehow, I knew what the next step would be. Sure enough, within the hour, Opperman called and asked if he could come right over. He had something to discuss.

I'd never seen him so apprehensive. His habitual assurance had been shaken. He paced back and forth for a few minutes and then came directly to the point. He wanted me to give his nominating speech. Since I had been expecting that, I'd given it some hurried thought. I knew the people who had threatened Bill, and I supposed that their vendetta was easily transferable to me. That was what did it, I guess. No one likes to be intimidated. I told Opperman that I'd be pleased to place his name in nomination.

He looked as if the warden had just granted full reprieve. He shook my hand. He recited his renewed resolve to forge in victory a party in which all were welcome. I'd heard that line so many times before, but now I could contrast it with the one example of iniquity to which I'd personally been exposed. Whether or not the students could bring about the intraparty harmony of which they spoke so often, they would at least conduct themselves above the vicious level of those who had intimidated Bill. That was something to look forward to.

4

The caucus was held on a Tuesday. I had thought March 5 would never come. And when it did the hours seemed protracted past endurance as I watched the lingering clock and apprehensively rehearsed my speech.

By late afternoon I returned home to shave a second time and change my shirt. I was interrupted in both functions by telephoned promptings to be sure to attend my caucus and support the McCarthy slate. The phone had been ringing with reminders for days. There must have been a dozen calls in all. And mail, too. A letter had been sent out over the signature of both Opperman and my young friend Katy, whom the steering committee had named as the ward candidate for chairwoman. (She was only twenty, but by November would be twenty-one and so could legally run for party office.) The peace movement appeared to be played down considerably. Instead, the letter pushed the unity theme with typical abandon; it was as ecumenical as anything I've seen.

There was also a letter from Nemerov. Its opening tone was ominous, if not downright alarming. The basic theme was that an irresponsible and destructive minority was trying to take over the ward and thereby destroy the humanitarian programs which others had implanted there. I wondered how many letters Nemerov had sent out. It was hard to believe that his mailing list could be as extensive as the students'—not after all those months of canvassing. Nemerov's campaign for the chairmanship was more of a last-minute effort.

The caucus was called for seven o'clock in the main ballroom of the Nicollet Hotel. This was only a block from my apartment, but my brother and I had accepted a dinner invitation from Katy and Joel before the caucus, so we drove over to their duplex on the West Bank.

My brother and Joel were calm and relaxed, which left just two nervous wrecks. I confess I was shaking a little when I arrived, speech cards in hand, but in contrast to Katy I was granite. She's high-strung by nature and the prospect of her imminent election contest wasn't helping. Nor was the fact that she'd accepted without reservation every possible canard and rumor about what Nemerov might have in storage for the evening. These she shared in full detail: Nemerov was at that very moment holding open house in a suite at the Nicollet, dispensing vast quantities of food and drink to all who would support his slate; his minions were combing the downtown bars for caucus votes; he was prepared to challenge every student's legal right to take part in the caucus; he was bringing a crew of strong-arm men to control things by brute force if necessary. I found this last charge particularly disturbing in light of my role as Bill Mullin's surrogate.

The dinner was not a success. I'm told that Katy burned the meat, but I really don't remember. My only vivid memory is of my hostess's agitation. She was so anxious that her friends get through.

We all drove over together in my car. The Nicollet Hotel, which had been selected by the Opperman faction as the caucus site, was located on the western boundary of the ward, as far from the main areas of population as one could get. Residents of my apartment house were the only ones within walking distance. Everyone else had to drive. This would prevent many older residents of the ward from participating.

At first I thought that this location was contrary to the students' interests, too. But I was wrong. No sooner had we pulled out onto the road when I began to notice cars with numbers on their sides. Big, painted numbers—7, 9, 4—attached by tape to each car door. Katy told me that this was all part of an elaborate car-pool operation that had been worked out some time before. Students were told to wait at certain pickup points for the car with their assigned number. It was very impressive. But as we moved on toward the caucus—flanked by a red six and a blue eleven—I couldn't help thinking of all the elderly voters trapped that evening in the senior citizen highrise apartments at the other end of the ward.

We parked near the Nicollet and went in. It was almost ten to seven, and I wondered how many people there would be. And who they would be for. We walked up to the ballroom on the mezzanine level and joined a small line to register at the door. No one challenged Joel or Katy's right to be there.

When I finally got into the ballroom the first thing I saw was Sue Opperman, handing out literature. The second thing I saw was a group of older people. A very large group. For a second that was all I saw. Dozens of people, none under fifty, standing near the door and talking to each other. Had Nemerov been able in just a few short weeks to mobilize so large a force? I remember my surprise.

And I remember my concern. If I hadn't really known it before, I knew it now: I wanted those students to win. I wanted that so badly. Not for seven of them to be delegates; that was something else. I wanted them to be allowed to continue the leadership of the ward they had been leading. I wanted them to have the officers' posts which they'd already earned with months of single-minded effort. I wanted them to know that all their work would bring results. I wanted them to *win*.

Then as I moved throughout the hall I saw some younger faces. The more I looked the more of them I saw. I paced off the ballroom from one end to the other. There were a lot of students, though it was hard to gauge whether they outnumbered the others. The reason that I hadn't sensed their presence at the outset was that their physical appearance had been altered for the evening. This was the first "Clean for Gene" occasion in the country. Everyone was well scrubbed and conventionally clad. Ties and jackets were the rule for young men, and not even the girls were wearing beads. Only Jock remained aloof from this tactic of display. His clothes and his hair were as defiant as ever.

Just before seven, large floodlights were snapped on at several places in the hall. I saw the mobile TV camera and some press reporters, too. They couldn't cover all the caucuses in other parts of town and so apparently had settled on the Sixth Ward for their story. Opperman had already received so much personal publicity; the reporters must have felt this was the place to be. Some looked disappointed at the crowd's well-dressed docility, and I saw a camera moving in to get at least a shot of Jock.

It was time to take our seats. There must have been a thousand folding chairs set up; they covered almost all the ballroom space. Each person had to sit with his own precinct, and it took me several minutes to find mine. Our chairs were in the farthest corner of the room, a good football field away from the podium. It seems this was no accident. The seating had been carefully arranged. The student precincts had been given the best positions on the floor. They were proximate to the speaker's platform but sufficiently spread out so that applause would come from every side. Opperman had been in charge of the arrangements.

And apparently he'd felt that my precinct was not friendly. That's why we had been placed at the very back of the hall. Almost every resident of the precinct lives in my apartment complex, where the rent is the highest in town. Our affluence, however conjectural, had cost us a good view of the proceedings.

I heard a gavel rapping in the distance and by squinting at the far-off rostrum I was able to recognize Opperman. He seemed to have had a hair cut recently; his hair looked shorter than before. And his boots had been replaced by shoes, well-shined. As Ward Club Chairman he was calling the meeting to order. But he would not conduct it: he explained at some length that he was disqualifying himself from the prerogative because of the advantage such exposure might give his candidacy. Someone else would chair the caucus.

The ward caucus, that is. First we had to conduct our separate precinct caucuses. Each precinct captain was in charge of that. No one was sure just who that was, but Bill Mullin did the honors. He explained, and very well I thought, just what it was we were to do.

There were fifty-four of us from our precinct. That was an unprecedented turnout from an apartment house regarded as predominantly Republican. I was among the youngest there.

Our first order of business was to elect a new precinct captain. As nominations were being entertained, blue sheets of paper were passed out to each of us. These lists, which had been prepared by the Opperman organization, were verbally described as the "Peace Slate," though they bore only the title "6th Ward DFL Slate." As I looked throughout the room I saw a rippled tide of blue passing through the other precincts. Each sheet listed various candidates for the various offices, carefully tailored to fit each particular precinct. If you were for peace, you were supposed to vote for the names on the blue paper.

The Peace Slate candidate for captain of my precinct was a good friend of mine, Jim Kaplan. He and his wife lived four floors down and two apartments over. He was a sports reporter for the afternoon paper, a liberal who had gone to Yale and strongly supported McCarthy for President.

Nemerov had a slate, too, at least in my precinct, which was his also. I don't think that his group had prepared detailed slates for all the other precincts, as Opperman had. It would have taken an enormous amount of work.

For precinct captain, the Nemerov candidate was Nemerov. In fact, his name appeared quite often as my eyes traversed his slate.

We cast our votes by secret ballot, and Jim Kaplan won hands down. The outcome had not really been in doubt. Earlier, we had taken a straw vote in our precinct, McCarthy versus Johnson-Humphrey. The Senator had won by a count of forty-eight to six. Opperman need not have feared our precinct. The well-to-do were not in favor of the war. Even among the six of us who remained loyal to the Administration, at least two—my brother and I—were strongly opposed to the war. We even had a name for it then, "Administration Doves." The other four votes had been cast (secret ballots aren't too secret) by Bill Mullin and by three older citizens whose interest in the race was perhaps not wholly ideological—the mother of a lawyer who was close to Hubert Humphrey, the mother-in-law of Minnesota's Democratic National Committeewoman, and a top employee of Robert Short, the local millionaire and gadfly in the party whose own efforts in the past to win high public office had been noticeably less successful than his triumphs in trucking, hotels, and the Los Angeles Lakers. Short was also very close to Humphrey. But several of the many others in the precinct who had just cast straw votes for the opposing side were also, in the normal course of things, substantial supporters of Humphrey too. They were middle-aged and middle-class and moderate. And they were very much against the war in Vietnam.

The next order of business was to elect our precinct's delegates to the Hennepin County convention. Or, rather, our delegate. We were only entitled to one. The number of delegates allocated to each precinct was determined by the size of the DFL vote cast within that precinct in the last general election. My precinct had very few DFL voters, so it only got one delegate to the county convention.

And that was me. There was my name, surrounded by blue in the middle of the Peace Slate. Opperman had insisted on it, even though I told him I wasn't supporting McCarthy. But I *was* for peace, he pointed out, so it was all right. And I was for Opperman, too, at least for the post of ward chairman, which may have had something to do with it. He wanted me to give his speech.

Nemerov knew how to count, and after the straw vote he withdrew his name from the county delegate race. I was elected unanimously, the first time I'd ever been elected to anything in the DFL. It felt very good. Jim Kaplan shook my hand and gave me my official delegate's card.

Throughout the ballroom the other precincts were electing their delegates, too. Some could choose as many as eleven. Together, the ward would elect one hundred and thirty-eight. The process went faster in some precincts than in others, the convoy moves no faster than its slowest ship. After more than an hour the precinct caucuses were declared closed by the Chair.

We were now one ward convention, not a disassociated group of precinct caucuses. The hundreds of people in the hall now had a single focus. They were about to begin what they had come there for.

The first order of business was the appointment of the tellers, who would sit up front and count the votes. Each side—Nemerov and Opperman—was allowed to choose half the tellers. Nemerov's were called by name and shuffled up to the platform. Central Casting would not have done it better. They looked like longshoremen ought to look if they are overweight and angry and about to do a job that has its risks. Then Opperman's tellers were called and they went up to the platform too. They were calm and poised and quiet. And all of them were nuns. For several seconds there was no response at all. Then the students started laughing, everywhere in the hall. There was even some applause. I had to hand it to Opperman.

The Chair called for order and got it. The crowded room was very still.

We had to elect ward officers before we could move on to choosing state convention delegates. We would elect the chairman and chairwoman first, then take the other officer slots in turn. The Chair announced that nominations were in order.

A lady near the front microphone stood up and placed in nomination the names of Irv Nemerov and his candidate for chairwoman. Then there was silence. We all just sat there. The Chair asked if there were any further nominations. There was no response. Just more silence. And then whispers. Several students turned their heads and looked around the room. They seemed to be looking at me.

Opperman had planned things so carefully, but he had forgotten one detail. He must have assumed that I knew as much about these proceedings as he. So no one had told me, or anyone else for that matter, that somebody had to place the name in nomination. Since this was my first caucus, I didn't know that this task was traditionally performed by whoever was to give the nominating speech. But given enough time, I figured it out. Just as even Katy was beginning to glare at me, the suspected traitor, I walked up to the front and placed Opperman's name and hers in nomination. Then I returned across the room to my seat.

As I rejoined my precinct, I received a funny look from the man who works for Robert Short. I assumed he was amused at the tardiness of my whole performance.

The first speech was for Nemerov. A stout lady slowly took the platform and commenced with her address. She was an accomplished speaker, though somewhat short on specifics. Her theme was hard to follow. She talked a lot about the London Blitz, of which apparently she'd been a victim. The allusion was surely to the present war and the need for its maintenance. Her description of her own lung ailment was rendered less effective than might otherwise have been the case had her delivery but been less forceful. I'll say this, she never insulted the students. She finished to quite respectable applause.

Now it was my turn, and I was no longer dilatory. I hurried right up to the lectern. As I faced the lights and shuffled my cards I had my first good look at the crowd. Just a glance, really, and I saw as many old faces as young. All of them were waiting.

I'm quite sure that my speech did not change any votes. But I tried to tell what the students had done. I spoke from personal experience of their phenomenal efforts within the political system. I described how they had revitalized the Ward Club. I tried to convey how much they had accomplished, how tragic, how unfair, how really unacceptable it would be now to refuse them formal leadership of what hard work had already made their own.

The time had come to justify the reason I had been asked to speak, and so, to reach the older people, I said that while all of us should vote for Opperman for chairman, I was one of those who on the later vote for state delegates would be supporting the Administration slate. I don't know whether this won over any elders, but it certainly elicited boos and shouts from many students. I quickly returned to the theme of electing students to the officer posts. That, I emphasized, was something on which all of us must surely agree. I poured it on as well as I knew how and finished to a long ovation which, beyond all doubt or ego, was more a measure of the students' fervor for their own cause than for my own expression of it.

We voted by secret ballot. As the disparate tellers worked at counting the result, nominating speeches were delivered for some of the lesser officer posts. These did not receive the rapt attention of the crowd. The vote would be almost the same on every officer position. But what would that vote be? The room grew loud with conversation. Several people asked for my prediction (having spoken, I was now an expert) but I really didn't know. Even if people had voted solely with their age group, it was hard to see from looking at the crowd just what the result would finally be. Even Opperman had grown quite pale.

But finally we had our answer. The Chair called for order and then waited with maddening slowness until every single voice was stilled. Only then did we hear the results.

The vote was incredibly one-sided. It was Opperman, 513; Nemerov, 137. It was a rout.

I've never heard such happy cheers as from those students. I've never felt a mood so free and jubilant. More than anything else, there was a great transcendent surge of pure relief. It was almost palpable, you could sense it. They were *relieved.* Yes, they'd worked so hard for many months and hoped so much for victory, too, but now one knew beyond all doubt how much they'd feared as well. They'd been afraid not merely of defeat; their dread had been not of one single loss but of the possibility that loss was the foregone conclusion. Their fear was the fear of daring to believe in the way things really ought to be. On blind and blunted trust alone, almost crippled with the burden of suspicion, they had set out to play it by the book. So their relief encompassed an entire system. That system worked. It worked for them. They'd won.

Things happened very quickly after that. First there was

the marked departure of many who had voted for the losing side. They knew how much they were in the minority and saw no binding reason not to leave. Then the Chair began to read the next results, which had been cast while we were waiting for the first. They told the same story. Then formalistic repetition of the balloting for all remaining offices. Then the call for a brief recess. Then Nemerov, with half his people out the door already, got up and publicly withdrew his entire slate of delegates.

It was all over. The McCarthy slate of delegates was unanimously elected. Seven McCarthy delegates to the state convention, Opperman, Kaibel, and five of their friends.

There was cheering this time, too, but somewhat more restrained. I think the students wanted the satisfaction of a real contest. I think they wanted Nemerov to stay in; though his departure seemed to me most prudent.

We were out of our seats, talking and laughing and waiting for the final gavel. But then, just after we had formally adjourned, somebody took the microphone and said to wait, there was an important announcement. He had just been on the phone, the results were in from the Eighth Ward. It had gone for McCarthy. All the delegates. The officers, too.

The outburst was louder than ever before. No one had expected this. It was remarkable. The Eighth Ward had few students; it was considered safe territory for the Administration forces. People were talking excitedly. If the Eighth Ward had gone McCarthy, then maybe, just maybe, the city might, too. The whole Fifth District, five delegate votes to Chicago. The prospect was agonizing. Several students went to look for phones to call the other wards. But most of the city caucuses were still going on. The students decided to go over to the Sixth Ward office and wait for the results there.

I was worried that they'd let their hopes become too high. I didn't want them to be too disappointed, not after this. Although I supposed that it *was* possible for them to carry the city. The McCarthy votes at our own caucus had not come only from students. They couldn't have, there weren't that many of them. Just look at my own precinct. I found myself anxious, too, to learn the city-wide results. But those, I knew, would not be complete for several hours.

I walked over to congratulate a young man I knew from ward club meetings who had been elected one of our seven delegates. I shook his hand, and he thanked me for giving Opperman's speech.

"Isn't it wonderful," I offered, "how well things turned out."

"Yes," he agreed, "but if those bastards had tried anything funny, well, we were ready for them." He opened his jacket and showed me a gun.

A gun. A dark gray revolver. He had a gun at our caucus. Oh my God, I thought, a gun. He really had a loaded gun.

I said nothing. There was nothing to say. I couldn't believe it. The young man did not seem to notice my distress. He shook my hand again and smiled and left.

I went over to my brother and told him what I'd seen. He couldn't believe it either. Then we were caught up again in the swirl of excited and happy students, and I tried to put the incident out of my mind.

We were invited to go with them all to their headquarters on the West Bank and join in the wait for results. I said that we'd be there later; I'd go first to the Johnson-Humphrey office and see what returns had come in there.

The Administration headquarters was less than a mile away. It took us only a few minutes to drive there. I was surprised that the street was so deserted; I had expected to have trouble parking. This was the best place in town to get the fresh returns. But there was no one in sight in any direction as we walked from the car to the door.

The headquarters was brightly lit, but there was almost no one there. Exactly four people greeted us as we came in. They were standing by a table in the middle of the room: Wendell Anderson, the State Campaign Chairman; Warren Spannaus, the DFL Chairman; Mike Berman, the Mondale aide from Washington; and Fred Gates, who was Hubert Humphrey's closest friend.

If courage is grace under pressure, then it was a very courageous quartet. Two of them were ashen gray but all smiled and were cordial. When they weren't smiling though, their lips were tightly drawn.

A few others wandered in, Bill Mullin among them, but most left after only a few minutes. There were never more than a dozen in the room at any time. And there was really nothing to see. There was a blackboard, ready for results, but this told very little. Only a few returns had been written in. There was the Sixth Ward, and the Eighth, and the Second. All were tabulated in the McCarthy column. But the Sixth and the Second were not surprising. And there was one ward, with quite a few state delegates, which had gone safely for Johnson-Humphrey. Most of the wards were still out.

That's what was so surprising. There was really very little evidence to base it on, but somehow you just *knew* that the Administration side had lost. You didn't have to wait for the results. You knew what they would be. I don't understand what chemistry pervades the air of an election night and instills in the politicos a sense of what will be. But it's there, it happens. Without facts, without proof, based only on a sudden certain sense, somehow the party regulars had known enough to stay away.

Gradually, from phone calls and personal visits, the facts began to confirm the pre-awareness. The McCarthy column grew longer and longer. The Ninth Ward had gone for McCarthy, the Thirteenth, the Seventh. And half the delegates from the Fifth Ward. The Fifth Ward! That's where I used to live, that's where I used to think the liberals never had a chance. That's where in other party fights I'd never even tried. And half the Ward had gone for Gene McCarthy.

The party leaders stayed at their table and watched the trenchant blackboard. They were frozen and immobile like the figures in the photos of some major summit conference. The silent men around the table showed no sign of what they felt. But the results kept coming in. It was an act of kindness to leave.

My brother and I drove over to the Sixth Ward office on the West Bank. Two blocks away we heard the celebration. One block away we saw it. They were crowded in the street. The office couldn't hold them all. Somewhere a radio was playing rock full-blast, but the sound of vocal celebration dominated the evening air.

It took a while to work our way inside. Many students still congratulated me for having nominated Opperman. But I didn't feel a part of what was going on. I was happy for them, but it wasn't my victory. It was theirs.

I was not alone in that view. Howie Kaibel threw me a triumphant smirk which brooked no doubt about whose side I had been on. Several others felt that way, too. Not all the greetings were friendly as I slowly edged my way through the crush toward the command post in the rear. There, from a radio just barely audible through the reveling, I learned the full, broad measure of the conquest.

The McCarthy forces had won a victory far beyond anyone's wildest predictions. They had a majority of the Fifth District, full control. And the Third and the Fourth Districts, too. They'd carried these by even greater margins than the Fifth. It had been almost a clean sweep in the suburbs and St. Paul. Three districts meant fifteen certain delegates to Chicago.

And it might mean much more. The First District returns were not in yet. The First District, which covered much of southern, rural Minnesota, I'd never even heard mentioned as a possibility before. Yet, scattered returns showed that it might go for McCarthy. It was hard to tell, it was very close.

If the First District delegates should be within the McCarthy camp, then that would be four congressional districts in all. Four out of eight. Four districts was not only twenty delegates to Chicago; it was half of the state convention. Not exactly half, that depended on the breakdown in each district, the total of how many wards and counties had been won. It could be less than half. And it could be more. If it *was* more, if the McCarthy delegates controlled the state convention, then they could and would elect all twenty at-large delegates to the Democratic National Convention. That would be forty

51

delegates to Chicago, by far the majority of Minnesota's delegation. The most for which the Johnson-Humphrey people could then hope would be a total of twenty-two delegates.

The possibility was very clear. The radio reports from the First District were coming in more steadily now, and the students became increasingly encouraged. Those students who were listening in, that is. Most couldn't hear through the din and so devoted themselves instead to having a very good time.

Vance Opperman was listening, though. He seemed to have the results before anyone else. I had difficulty getting his attention, he seemed so intensely preoccupied. When he did focus in on me, he asked if I remembered that he'd put one girl to work in the Twelfth Ward. I answered yes. He told me the results of her efforts: half the Twelfth had just been won for McCarthy, a stronghold bisected by a single girl on the phone. Opperman should have been ecstatic, but he was too busy for emotion. He kept counting precinct delegates to the county convention. He had his own chart for these, and soon he returned to it, completely engrossed by what he saw.

I didn't want to bother him any further, or anyone else that evening either. More than ever I felt my status as outsider. As it ought to be, I thought, considering the still growing success of a movement now state-wide in scope, which I had not supported. Why shouldn't they celebrate, why shouldn't they be drawn together at this ascendant moment? If McCarthy was to have most of our state delegates, then he —then those who'd worked for him—had won them fair and square. Let them have what they had won. And let them revel in their own achievement. It had been earned. Now they could spend their gains as well—not just in Chicago, but here at home. The infusion of energy and spirit could mobilize the DFL as well, mobilize and strengthen and expand the party base. It was a happy thought.

5

The next morning turned out to be very busy, and not at all the way I'd planned. I remember walking to my office. I felt incredibly good. All that politicking had ended rather well. And it *had* ended. That was the best part. I could get back to whatever it is I'm supposed to do for a living.

I walked into the lobby of the Midland Bank Building, where I have my office, and stood waiting for an elevator. Nearby, with the morning paper in his hand, well-dressed as always, was a friend of my parents who worked in the same building. He was a courtly gentleman, Yale Law '24, distinguished in both profession and public service. Despite the difference in our ages, he was always very cordial when we met. Now I saw that he was reading about last night's caucuses. As we got into the elevator, I asked him what he thought about it all.

He was delighted with the results. He told me that he'd attended his own caucus in the suburbs and had enthusiastically supported the McCarthy slate. He'd made sure that his wife, his daughter, and his son-in-law went, too. This kind of political activity was unusual for him, he related, which is just what I was thinking. He seldom became that involved. I asked who had recruited him to come out and participate. "No one," he answered. He'd heard or read somewhere that the caucuses would be held on Tuesday night, and when Tuesday night came he simply got up and went.

"It was the war," he explained, "that stupid, pointless war. It's about time we did something about it." And so he'd brought out his family to their caucus. Where they prevailed. He told me the margin his side had won by, and I realized that it was even greater than Opperman's victory in the Sixth

Ward. And apparently in his suburb there had been almost no prior organizing efforts. Most of those who turned out were just like him, decent people, not very political, who didn't like the war. I thought of all the older people in my own precinct who had felt and voted the same way. It was becoming clear that the students' feverish campaign accounted for only a small part of the massive McCarthy victory. The elderly partisan at my side was in the normal course of things an ardent Humphrey supporter.

As we reached his floor, I made some comment about this being an exciting year. He looked bemused.

"There's a good script," he suggested, "but the cast is wrong. If McCarthy was the Vice-President, and if Humphrey was leading the charge, now *that's* what I'd call an exciting year. What a shame they can't switch places." The doors closed behind him.

I got to my office, but not to my work. The answering service told me to call Warren Spannaus, the DFL State Chairman. I'd known Warren since we started out together in the attorney general's office, so when I returned his call I assumed that he just wanted to talk about the caucus results. I was wrong.

"You're in trouble," he said, "Short's really uptight."

For a second I thought he was talking about underwear. Warren quickly dispelled my confusion. It seems Bob Short had called him, enraged. At me. Short's employee who lived in my precinct presumably had reported my activities on behalf of the student officer slate. I couldn't imagine why Short found this so upsetting, but his reaction, according to Warren, was explosive.

"He called you a fat, swarthy bastard," Spannaus said.

Now that hurt. My skin is of an average pallor, and so I have no hangups on the subject, but my weight is something else again. I was fifteen pounds too heavy and very touchy about it. I didn't like being called fat. And I was mad that Short was mad. I scarcely knew him. What business was it of his whom I chose to nominate? Upon reflection, I decided that it might be the hotel business. Short's hotels were in the

Sixth Ward, and their destiny was to some extent in the hands of the Sixth Ward alderman. I guess the theory was that whoever controlled the ward club controlled the endorsement of a DFL candidate for alderman. I could understand why Short would be interested in this decision and angry that it would now be made by people he didn't know.

What I didn't realize was how many other people were experiencing a similar reaction: their party was now in the hands of strangers. This was true throughout the Twin Cities metropolitan area, in three congressional districts. As party regulars learned the scope of the McCarthy victory they also grasped the fact that it was not a victory of those whom they knew personally. And they found this most distressing. For a variety of reasons, the party regulars wanted to talk with the new leadership, but they weren't too sure just who that was. The papers were giving much of the credit to the students, even though many of the most lopsided margins were in areas which the students hadn't even tried to organize. But political insiders are as susceptible to what they read in the newspapers as is the general public, perhaps more so. At least they read the political news more carefully. What they read about this morning was students, and what they wondered was how to find out more about them. Whom did they know who knew, in turn, these student activists?

That's why my morning was busy. Guess who they knew. It seems that the night before, the Sixth Ward caucus had been one of the few to finish in time for the television men to get their film ready for the ten o'clock news. My nominating speech, without sound, was shown as background to the announcer's tabulation of results. Minneapolis isn't that large a place; a lot of the party regulars knew me, they recognized me in the TV clip. Surrounded by students.

So my phone began to ring. It rang all morning. By noon I'd spoken with a very good cross section of the urban DFL, including several elected officials whom I'd always wanted to meet. They seemed to regard me as an expert on the Sixth Ward students, a status quite unjustified and highly ironic as well, since, with no better basis in fact, I had until then been regarded by the Sixth Ward students as an expert on the party regulars. Each side certainly had misjudged my familiarity with the other. The party regulars were frantic for information. They all asked the same questions—what was Opperman like, were the students (the word never varied) "reasonable," and were they only interested in national convention delegates, or would they try and take over the state party too. This last query bothered me. I pointed out that the students were very publicly committed to an open party in which all could participate. It was delegates they were after. That was all. Just ask them. They were basically a peace movement. But no matter how many times I repeated this, most of my callers remained pretty skeptical.

By late afternoon the focus of the calls had changed from inquiry to solicitation. Several people called to enlist my support in working the farm areas on behalf of the Administration forces. The rural equivalent of the ward caucus was the county convention. These chose state delegates just as the wards did. But they chose them later in time—three and four and in some cases five weeks later. The precinct delegates had already been chosen in the rural areas, and now they just had to wait until their county conventions came up; the dates varied from county to county. The important thing was that these precinct delegates had been selected, they were *identified,* their names were filed with the state DFL office, and there was still time to reach them.

Time for both sides to reach them. That was the problem. The students had won in the cities and the suburbs. Now they were free to work the rural areas, too. And not randomly, door-to-door. If they had possession of these new precinct delegate lists, their trips to the country could be most direct. They would know just whom to see.

From the earlier calls, I had received the impression that the party regulars vastly overrated the scope and the impact of the student effort. This second batch of calls removed all doubt. Some of the older party members imagined a vast and energetic student organization capable of stampeding the countryside into their camp. They were very worried; in fact, they were terrified. It reminded me a little of the students themselves, so fearful, prior to the caucuses, of a huge and largely mythical machine which organized labor was supposed to be mobilizing against them. On neither occasion had I joined in the concern. I didn't think now that the rural precinct delegates would be very susceptible to the kind of movement which had worked so successfully in the cities. I didn't think that the party regulars were justified in trying so desperately to stop it.

And I didn't intend to help them. I had already devoted more time than I could afford to local politics. Enough was enough. It was doubtful whether the rural delegates would find me charismatic. And, more to the point, I couldn't bring myself to tell anyone to support the war. I suppose I could tell them to do what I had done—oppose the war but support the Administration, too. And at the same time push for the best party officers from each side. But I knew that my own convoluted approach to the matter would be difficult to explain very quickly to others. It was beginning to sound dubious even to me. No, in winning over delegates there was no time for subtle distinctions. You were selling the whole ball of wax. You were selling just one slate. You were selling the war. I just couldn't do it.

So to each request for help I found some excuse for declining. This wasn't always easy; my callers were persistent. They seemed to feel that they needed all the help they could get. It was hard to put them off, but I made the effort. I said I had to try a case. I said I had to be out of town. I said I had a deadline for filing a brief in court. I succeeded in putting them off for a time, but I'd won only a delay, not a reprieve. The calls kept coming in.

All this was during just one day, the day after the caucuses. What a frenzy of activity from the Administration side. They were motivated at last. And I think I know what was motivating them—their pride, which had been severely wounded. As I looked at the afternoon paper—the whole front page was devoted to the caucus results—I scanned long lists of names of former party leaders who had not been permitted to be even precinct delegates. Party leaders, labor leaders, elected officials, mayors, aldermen, state legislators, had not been allowed to represent their precincts at our own upcoming county convention. I regarded this as some kind of mistake. It couldn't be intentional. Unlike the rural county meetings coming up, the Hennepin County convention had nothing to do with the process of selecting national convention delegates. I couldn't see why some of the party regulars should not have been sent there as delegates from their precincts. It was the minimal post one could obtain within the party. But Administration supporters had been shut out of the precinct delegate spots wherever they were in the minority. In the Sixth Ward, for example, I was virtually the only Administration supporter out of 138 delegates to the Hennepin County convention. It seemed ridiculous to deny these token spots—they could have no effect on the peace movement—to so many people who had worked hard over the years to help elect the party's candidates. It was pointless to insult people; no principle was served by angering them.

And they were angry. Their names were in the paper as losers, their pride was really hurt. Several of my callers had been particularly upset because of the reasons given publicly for their defeat. It wasn't just losing, it was the fact that, very frequently, they had been insulted as well. Some of the rhetoric was most unfortunate. In all too many precincts where the McCarthy voters were in control, the Administration minority had been told that they could not even be precinct delegates because they were fascists, warmongers, immoral. This didn't strike me as a very good way for the McCarthy movement to consolidate its gains. The charges they made, the language they used, were childish. And, of course, many of the villified Administration people had been opponents of the war themselves for quite some time. It was still less than twenty-four hours since the caucuses had ended, and already I was tired of the name-calling. (On reflection, I thought I'd rather be called a fat bastard than a fascist pig.)

I noticed, too, that the afternoon paper, the Minneapolis *Star*, was certainly hammering home the theme that the McCarthy victory had been accomplished by the very young. The lead story stated that "much of the muscle behind the McCarthy drive in Minneapolis was supplied by University of Minnesota students and former students in the West Bank section of the Sixth Ward." Opperman and Kaibel were singled out for their efforts. And in the same paper there was an editorial entitled "DFL Jolt For Johnson-Humphrey," in which the word "young" was the invariable adjective. The "outpouring of young McCarthyites," the "tactics of the young adults," were looked upon approvingly. The morning paper had said the same things: "Mobilized largely by young people urging an end to the war in Vietnam, metropolitan voters swept . . ." Which was just fine. But I couldn't help thinking of the man I'd met on the elevator that morning. He was nearly seventy. From firsthand and admiring observation, I knew full well how hard the students had worked. They deserved much credit, but they were only one part of the McCarthy movement, a minority it seemed to me. The reports in the paper, the phone calls that had been coming in all day, the facts of my own caucus, indicated that a good deal of last night's success had been the spontaneous reaction of a disaffected populace, prompted not by student organizers but purely by their own concern. I thought again of the elderly lawyer who had gone to his caucus to protest the war. I suspected that he was as good a symbol as any of the victory which others were ascribing to the young. I hoped so, because I wanted to believe that the victory encompassed the mood of many people of all ages. I didn't want to feel that it had somehow been imposed upon the populace through organization and effort and computers and phone calls, however worthy these tactics might be. I wanted to think of it as the natural response of a concern which was already there, a concern which had been consciously directed by a host of individuals to precisely the place where it would do the most good—their precinct caucuses. That's the way the system is supposed to work. And now there could be no doubt that that is the way it *had* worked. Those who wished to praise the McCarthy movement should have stressed this fact above all else, for it reflects far more credit on their cause and on the system which made it possible, than can the narrow focus on one small group of youth alone. The real story seemed to me far greater than the one being told.

For the moment, however, attention shifted from the victory's meaning to its scope. The final results were still not in. The following day, Thursday, which as before I had begun with the dim hope of getting back to work, brought another front-page headline, "McCarthy Forces Claim 1st District." It was only a claim, of course, but it doubled the number of phone calls asking, sometimes now demanding, that I join the effort to stem the McCarthy tide in the rural conventions. I knew the arguments very well. The loss of the First District would be the loss of the state. I rather doubted whether this would happen, but I must say that the McCarthy delegate claims were disputed very cautiously indeed by the Administration spokesmen. So maybe it was true. We wouldn't know until the county conventions. But I maintained my resolve to stay away from these. The entreaties became so frequent that I wondered whether I shouldn't just leave the phone off the hook.

One call, though, was for another purpose. Congressman Fraser's office wanted to know if I could attend a luncheon the next day in which the impact of the caucuses would be examined. I said I'd be pleased to be there, and I meant it. I had the feeling that emotions were beginning to get out of hand. It would be helpful to get together and restore a sense of perspective. I though that Fraser was wise to call the meeting.

Warren Spannaus disagreed. The Party Chairman called me that afternoon and said that he'd been invited to the luncheon, too, but that he planned to stay away. He thought the meeting was a mistake. It was a bad idea to try to get both sides together so soon after a decisive political fight. It was better to allow a cooling-off period. That struck me as a little overcautious. I wasn't as close to the situation as he was; I didn't know what there was to cool off. Just how wise Warren was remained to be seen.

It was seen the next day. I walked over to the Pick-Nicollet Hotel at noon on Friday and looked at the schedule board in the lobby to see where Fraser's lunch would be. It wasn't listed. But I asked at the desk and was directed to a private dining room on the mezzanine.

We met at a u-shaped conference table, with places set for about twenty. I was one of the first to arrive, so I had a drink and watched the others come in. I figured I had been invited as a courtesy because of some fund-raising I'd done in the Fraser campaign, and I wondered who else would be at the meeting. As the room filled up I recognized a number of people, someone from just about every ward, it seemed. Several faces were new to me. One thing, though, about the guests: you didn't have to know any of them to figure out which side they'd been on three nights earlier. You would have had to be blind not to be able to tell the McCarthy supporters from the Administration supporters, just from the looks on their faces. In fact, a blind man *could* have made the same distinction, if he listened very carefully; the Administration supporters weren't doing any talking. It was the faces, though, which told the story best. How easy it would be to say that each face transmitted either victory or defeat, but it wasn't quite that simple. Each face showed a mixture of emotions. One group, clearly in the majority at that luncheon, exhibited a combination of jubilation, pride, and scorn. All the other visages were those of sullen ire. Haughty eyes met angry and defensive stares. It was clenched teeth versus the smirk.

The exception was our host. Congressman Fraser's features were, as always, ordered and intelligent, with that slight hint of cosmic bemusement which sets him above the ranks of his colleagues. He's one of only two men I know in public life who asks a question simply because he wants to learn the answer. If he noticed that his well-intentioned *déjeuner* was starting on a hostile note, he managed to conceal it. He surely felt no part of the division which was so apparent in the room. His own views throughout that year (about the same as mine, I proudly noted) represented an anguished sympathy with both sides. No one in the Congress had opposed the war more forcefully or for a longer time than Fraser. Yet he saw our national problems, particularly the issue of racial equality, as solvable only by a united and victorious Democratic party. So this most outspoken of doves was supporting the Administration and encouraging the dissent. Like me, he thought one could do both. That's why he'd called both sides to the same meeting. He seemed happy that everyone had come; he was anxious to hear what they had to say.

He got his chance. No sooner had the food been served than the guests were asked to rise in turn and speak their minds. I don't recall that anyone declined this opportunity.

I'll say this about the comments, they were memorable. Or perhaps unforgettable is slightly more precise. I know I'll never forget them. As speaker followed speaker, several thoughts occurred to me. The first was that Warren Spannaus was a very fine authority on the timing of luncheons. My second thought was that some people were certainly saying some very foolish things. Next, that I really should reread some Edmund Burke. Then I just got angry.

For the first half hour, only the McCarthy supporters did the talking. Their comments varied somewhat in tone, but they did have a common theme. Two themes, really. The first was that now they were totally in charge of the party. The second was that those who had not been with them were evil and could no longer be permitted to remain within the DFL. I regarded the first point as a miscalculation and the second as a disaster. There was no way of missing either one. A young architect delivered a long address about what he called the unhappy marriage of labor and liberals and announced that he was pleased at last to declare that the divorce was final. Vance Opperman, seated to my left, spoke in a very pleasant manner but managed nonetheless to suggest that unless Congressman Fraser publicly switched his support to McCarthy he might not be re-endorsed for office by the new party membership. At this point I joined the discussion, stating rather directly my views on the practice of threatening congressmen, particularly one whose opposition to the war had so long antedated that of those now attempting to intimidate him.

In response to my defense of Fraser I was treated to a little speech from a gentleman seated opposite me, a fellow I'd gone to law school with, who informed me with some unction that my tired old brand of "politics as usual" was gone forever. I was still too much of a novice to *have* a brand of politics, and "politics as usual" is not a phrase I've ever really understood, though one hears it often enough. If it means the frustration of democratic procedures, then I supported its demise, though I must say that I was becoming apprehensive about the new order of things as well. Whatever happened to all that talk before the caucuses about unity and fellowship and everyone working together? What goal was being served by all these gratuitous insults and threats and pompous verbal purges? I looked toward the end of the table where the other Administration supporters were sitting. One, an alderman, had already left. The others seemed angry, but they remained silent. I was appalled by the open arrogance of the victors. I was wishing that someone would try to restore a sense of perspective to what had become an ugly and pointless confrontation.

Someone did try. Sam Richardson, State Chairman of the NAACP, one of the few blacks to hold high office in the DFL, now beaten in his caucus fight, refrained from speaking until Fraser made a point of asking for his comments. Even then he spoke briefly, in a low voice. He talked about something which no one else had seen fit to mention—the ability of a party to win elections. He pointed out the distinction between getting control of the party apparatus—not very hard, in a state which has no bosses—and being able to win acceptance from the voters for that party and its candidates. And its principles. What good were all these words about a new day dawning, Richardson asked, if the party was to split itself, to antagonize its allies, to anger its voters, to lose the election? You could tell that he was trying to

63

keep emotion from his voice, but he didn't quite succeed. His despair was unmistakable. He could see what was coming.

So could the other blacks who were present at that luncheon. Several voiced the same concern. They didn't want to lose elections either. They were not so very eager to dismiss with a sneer the money and the votes and the support of organized labor, sometimes a reluctant ally but the strongest one they had. The issue of race and jobs and economic opportunity had never been mentioned by the brash young white professional men who had monopolized the meeting up until then. They didn't have to think about things like that. They didn't have to be concerned with losing an election. The outcome of a political contest would not change their way of life at all. The blacks, on the other hand, knew that the war was wrong, but life had let them in on other truths as well. They knew what difference it made if a liberal party won or lost. They knew who paid the price of defeat.

Out of courtesy to their color, no one disputed what they had to say. But I had the feeling that no one really listened either. The young white spokesmen seemed to regard these new remarks as just an interesting digression, a detail. The meeting resumed its prior tone, maintaining it to the end. Each group left separately.

I stayed behind to talk with Fraser. On my way to the luncheon, I had noticed that the executive council of the state AFL-CIO was meeting on the same floor of the hotel. I suggested to Fraser that he might want to drop by and greet the delegates. He was all for it, and together we went down the hall to the labor conference room. I went in to see if it was possible for Fraser to speak for a few minutes. It was not. An older officer of the state federation looked alarmed when I suggested it. He drew me aside and rasped some advice.

"Jesus Christ," he warned, "don't let Don even come in here. They'll skin him alive. They're so goddam mad they'll take it out on the first DFLer who walks in that door." I thanked him for the advice, which, judging from the look of the crowd, seemed very prudent indeed.

Fraser said nothing when I told him he couldn't go in, but he was obviously upset by the rejection. He's a strong supporter of labor legislation in Congress; I don't think anyone has a better voting record there. Labor always helps in his campaigns. And one of his most difficult campaigns was coming up, the Republicans having decided to make a serious effort to unseat him. He was a friend of most of the labor leaders behind those closed doors. He was a United States Congressman. And they wouldn't let him in. The union men had been to their caucuses, too, and had been called everything from pigs to hacks. They had been told that they were no longer wanted in the party, and for the time being they were glad to comply with the suggestion. It wasn't a question of the war; it was a matter of personal insult. Whatever had been said to them at their caucuses, it had been monumentally effective.

The most honorable men are always caught in the middle and that was Fraser's plight. Scarcely an hour before, he had been subtly threatened by Opperman because he wouldn't support McCarthy's campaign. Now, he was warned to stay out of a labor meeting whose members, in their anger and humiliation, might focus their rage upon an early opponent of the war, the representative of a party whose image in their eyes had undergone a very great change. And would change even more.

6 I don't know why I was so blind to what was going on. Perhaps it was because I had endorsed completely the students' first and finest premise that I was able to abate my natural concern for where their cause could lead them. Or who could lead them.

Even after the angry and arrogant meeting at the Nicollet, I still wasn't sure just where we were being driven. I attributed the excesses to youth and inexperience and to the first great heady encounter with political success. It was possible that tolerance might yet prevail.

The next few weeks took care of any doubts. Everything that could have happened, happened then. I learned a great deal, painfully.

For just a few welcome days the political talk ceased to be local; everyone was speculating on how McCarthy would do in the New Hampshire primary that coming Tuesday. People in Minneapolis were amused at the cautiousness of the national columnists and by the bland assumption of those pundits that this would be McCarthy's first political test. *We* had been his first political test, and he had won. He had won two cities and perhaps a state. In Minnesota no one asked whether McCarthy would do well in New Hampshire. Of course he would do well. The question was how well, and the floor on the betting was seldom less than 40 percent of the vote.

There was one week between the Minnesota caucuses and the New Hampshire primary. I've never understood why Robert Kennedy didn't rely on the facts of the first event in order to decide to enter the race before the second could occur. If he had announced his candidacy before New Hampshire, instead of three days later, he could have taken credit for much of the vote that McCarthy received there. By waiting, he seemed to the McCarthyites like a usurper. The two peace candidates could not avoid splitting their movement. More to the point, if Kennedy had announced before New Hampshire, his campaign would have been that much stronger from the start. Things might have turned out very differently. Of course, there was only a week between Minnesota and New Hampshire. That isn't much time. It may seem unreasonable, provincial even, to expect a national figure to make such a major judgment based on some caucuses in a Midwestern state. But if Kennedy had been in Minnesota that week, it's hard to believe that he would have missed the mood, discernible everywhere as absolute conviction, that the peace movement went far deeper and broader than the network commentators were even suggesting. The spontaneous outpouring at our caucuses had been too dramatic to deny. Yet no one outside our borders seemed to see it as a harbinger.

After New Hampshire, on March 13, the national political picture became much clearer to everyone. The full potential of the peace movement could at last be seen, which meant that back in Minnesota, our still unfolding battle was resumed with new intensity.

And with that new intensity, the bad feeling already all too evident could only get much worse. Amicability in politics apparently is possible only in the absence of a contest. We still had a very serious contest for control of the state party. Whatever contact had remained between the two factions was clearly less than amicable now.

A good example was the caucus lists. The same local newspaper which bore the headline "McCarthy Receives 41 Percent of N.H. Democratic Votes" also had a story titled "Pro-Johnson Officers in DFL Won't Reveal Delegate Names." Both sides were getting ready to court the rural delegates whose county conventions would not take place until the end of the month. In order to talk to these delegates, you had to know who they were. And their names were not unknown. They were listed on the official precinct caucus lists which had been forwarded from each county to the state DFL office. The lists were in that office—in a vault. They had been locked up for safekeeping, and the DFL Chairman announced that they would stay locked. Not forever, of course. Just until the party had had a chance to write its own letters of congratulations to the new county delegates. No one stated exactly how long it would take to write those letters. It could take until the end of the month.

The McCarthy organizers were furious. They were absolutely certain that this was a device to keep them from converting the rural delegates to their side. They demanded the lists. They pointed out that the lists had been made public in the past. They threatened to sue. The lists stayed locked up in the vault.

I didn't know about the precedents, but it seemed to me obvious that the McCarthy demands were justified in principle. And as a matter of practical strategy, they simply had to have those names.

For now the fight was truly joined. Each side could see a chance to win. Their claims conflicted so greatly that everyone knew the final vote would be terribly close. Hard work and organization could make the difference. But it was more than that. It was more than votes which were at stake. It was pride and anger and fear. The DFL officers were wrong in refusing to give out the delegate lists, but it wasn't hard to comprehend their mood of sharp recalcitrance. It had very little to do with the war. The party regulars had been exposed to unlimited derision and attack from the moment the city caucuses had ended. They had been told that they were through, regardless of their views or work on any other matter, including the war. If the McCarthyites won the state, then everyone else in the party was through. That had been made resoundingly clear. Thanks to public insults and to threats heaped upon them in the caucuses they saw themselves as fighting for their very survival. And they acted accordingly.

Perhaps nowhere as much as in politics does paranoia have the capacity to be so self-fulfilling. The worst suspicions give birth to exactly what they fear. If the McCarthyites had not regarded their caucus rivals as venal hacks and said so at every opportunity, then the party regulars might not have acted so atypically. In Minnesota, politics is usually a very open thing; few games are played. But now there was a list locked up in an iron safe. Extraordinary measures were the response to extraordinary behavior. The excesses of one side caused the other to behave badly, too. And once begun, this whole process of negative interaction slid into a downward spiral of accusation and chicanery. Each side reinforced the other in its least attractive aspects. It kept getting worse and worse.

At least there was no lack of interest in what we still could call the political process. No one talked of anything else but the upcoming battle for delegates. And my office phone resumed its series of summonses. This time party people had no patience with excuses. I was needed in Stearns County (my mother's birthplace) and I had better be there. By a combination of tenacity and guile, I succeeded in turning down any specific assignment. I was no longer very sympathetic with the students, but my views against the war remained the same. So somehow I avoided working in the field. It wasn't easy. My callers were pretty excited. They were terrified of the students' ability to organize. They really had the most exaggerated view of their opponents' strength, especially as regards the computer. The local press had written so much about the Sixth Ward computer operation that the party regulars saw it as already being on a par with IBM. The Minneapolis *Tribune,* in its efforts to explain the caucuses, had run an enormous background story headlined "Computer Helps Backers of McCarthy Alter DFL." The story began, "To some architects of the uprising against President Johnson, it is not Sen. Eugene J. McCarthy, but rather the computer, that will remake Minnesota's Democratic-Farmer-Labor party." There was a large picture of three students holding an endless computer print-out: Opperman, Kaibel, and the fellow who had shown me his gun. The story presented as fact some things that these leaders had told the reporter. I could see why the party regulars were impressed, as I read of Herculean accomplishment. Thirty-five thousand doorbells rung in the Sixth Ward alone, a vast army of volunteers, an amazingly sophisticated series of special mailings.

It was hard to recognize my ward club from the newspaper's description. Whenever I thought of the computer, I thought of the night I'd helped to program it with a handful of others from the ward. We hadn't completed very many names. In fact, Opperman had told me that only slightly more than a thousand canvassed names had ever been programmed at all. He openly laughed at what the papers were doing to the facts. I didn't think it was so funny. From the start, I'd felt that the press had found the wrong heroes. It was not just students who had triumphed at the caucuses—the wrong heroes and the wrong weapon. It was conscience, not some shiny new computer, which had been used to win that fight. Anyway, I suppose the real story was too abstract for a daily newspaper. That's nothing new. I'm sure that not every jobless man in the 1930s was actually engaged in selling apples, despite all the pictures to the contrary. But how else do you photograph a depression? And how else do you summarize and explain, simply and dramatically, a very extensive upheaval in a political party? You can't. The newspapers can't, anyway. At least not in Minneapolis. So they take a picture of a computer and of three young men who say things about it. And that explains everything.

The struggle which was really going on had its own dimension of savage intensity, and given the behavior of the spokesmen for each side, the mood was almost inevitable. The worst fights seem to come when both sides are in the right. And each side *was* right with regard to its own first concern. I'm not talking about leadership now, but of the average partisan in each camp. The McCarthy followers were right to oppose the war and to do so through the political process. The Administration supporters in Minnesota were right in seeing that if this particular group of opponents triumphed, they would destroy the party structure. They were right, too, in knowing what this meant. A political party ought not to be preserved for its own sake; its *raison d'être* lies in what it alone is able to achieve. Here is my square, unfashionable, pragmatic point of view: only a large political party, an institutionalized coalition of disparate, widespread membership, can mobilize the kind of support which results in the winning of elections. Winning elections is the only lever that the people really have, but it is the most powerful lever of all. Not just presidential elections. Parties are becoming less important there than the coaxial cable. I'm talking about all elections. Only a political party, organized and mobilized and very broadly based, can win the races for those local posts—alderman and governor and legislator and mayor—which in the aggregate can determine inimitably the course of our common destiny. The track record is very clear. If you don't care about political parties, then you don't care about civil rights or civil liberties or tax reform or pollution or the war or anything else. So both sides were right. One wanted to end the war, and the other wanted to preserve a liberal state party which is perhaps the most responsive in the nation.

The obvious question here is why we can't do both. Why can't there be a candidate, a movement, a populace, a cause, which wants to end the war, which wants to do the things which need to be done and at the same time recognizes that a viable and unified party is its best hope for achieving those goals? The obvious question has an obvious answer: there's no good reason why we can't have both. That's precisely what's so frustrating. There doesn't have to be a fight at all. You just have to stop being exclusionary.

The Kennedys knew this, it was the key to their success. In that sense, Robert Kennedy was the perfect candidate for 1968. But he had no campaign in Minnesota. He had wisely seen the futility of entering the state which had produced two major figures in the contest for the presidency.

And if Kennedy had entered Minnesota, I wonder how well he could have done. The elitism of the upper-middle class is a terrible barrier to cross. There are people who consider political strategy to be a base consideration. If they believe in a goal, and all their friends do, too, well, that really ought to be enough. They will not descend to the level of effectuating their beliefs. They *know* what is good; it would be demeaning to look for further support.

I remember the day that Robert Kennedy announced that he was entering the race for the presidency. Now, I think it's safe to say that Robert Kennedy was a better vote-getter than Eugene McCarthy. The polls all showed that. He had a better chance of beating Nixon. And he had a better chance of getting the endorsement; the Democratic regulars knew that no Kennedy is anti-party. They could support him and survive. And, of course, Kennedy was against the war. People who oppose the war should be concerned with ending it, and to most of the McCarthy supporters it must have been clear that Kennedy's chances of being president were far greater than McCarthy's.

I was so naïve that when I heard Kennedy's announcement I assumed it would cause rejoicing in the peace movement. The strongest candidate was on their side. Of course, I didn't expect that all of the students would rush to support him. I was learning that some of them had very specific plans which had nothing to do with the war. But the majority of the peace movement, the upper-middle class whose interest was primarily to get us out of Vietnam, I thought that they'd be happy now.

So when I called the Doctor's Wife I was for once expecting a conversation devoid of the word "immoral." And in the strictest possible sense, I was right. When I asked what she thought of Kennedy's getting into the race, she snapped back that she thought it was obscene.

"What?" I asked.

"Obscene," she said.

"Why?"

"Because it's just not fair. McCarthy started first. He *deserves* to have it. Why should Kennedy be able to benefit from another man's initial courage? McCarthy was there first. For Kennedy to come in now is just obscene."

With the benefit today of hindsight, I could easily overdramatize my point. For at the moment of this conversation an unstable young lieutenant by the name of Calley was approaching through the underbrush a village which his map called My Lai IV. That's true, but it's not fair. We didn't know that then. But we did know that a war was going on, a brutal, terrible war and that we both wanted nothing so much as for it to be ended. Or so I had thought.

But this nice, well-educated lady had something else in mind. She was the product of her class. Not just her social class, her kindergarten class as well. I could just see her at the age of five, out on that smooth playground with the other well-scrubbed kids. They were playing a game, and someone had tried to sneak in ahead of his turn. That wasn't fair. They knew it wasn't fair, that's what they'd always been taught, and they were right. Johnny started first, so we should let him finish. That was the good clean rule of her honest and productive life. Her voice even sounded like that of a child; it was so clear and simple and certain.

I tried to make some arguments, but it was plainly a waste of time. So I switched the subject slightly. The Doctor's Wife had become quite prominent in the local McCarthy movement. I asked her what we could do to lower the level of invective from both sides. She didn't regard the matter as being that important. She was more interested in winning over the rural delegates. I explained that that was precisely what I was talking about, too, but I'm afraid that we didn't get very far at all.

So the contest for delegates remained quite normal, which is to say that things became progressively worse. The first series of county conventions was scheduled for the last weekend in March, less than two weeks off. The afternoon paper, the Minneapolis *Star,* ran a feature story under the headline, "Partisans Say McCarthy Will Win Convention Vote." It was an accurate summary of the current McCarthy claims. The state convention would have 1,110 delegates. For control, 556 votes were needed. The McCarthy leadership said that it already had 400 state delegates absolutely committed. It hoped to pick up many more at the county conventions, enough for total control. This was not too unlikely. In addition to the three congressional districts they had already won, the McCarthyites insisted that the First District would be theirs, too. And now they even talked about carrying the Sixth. That was impressive. The Sixth District is largely rural. If they did well there, then it was all over. It seemed possible. The Sixth has a very large Catholic population. And it has the town of Watkins where Gene McCarthy was born and raised. He went to college at St. John's, near St. Cloud, also in the Sixth. Without doubt, it was going to be close.

I just assumed that since total victory was finally within sight, the student organizers would intensify their past activity. And they did, in a way. That very evening Opperman and his group met for many hours to make plans. I read about it in the paper. The plans they made, however, were not related to capturing the state for McCarthy. What they were planning was how to win Hennepin County for Opperman. It seems that what Opperman had wanted all along was to become a power in the party. He saw the Hennepin County chairmanship as his best and swiftest move. It suddenly became clear why, before the caucuses, he had spent so much time finding precinct delegates in wards which were sewed up for the Administration. No matter how the majority of the ward voted on the McCarthy slate to the state convention, each precinct remained free to send whomever it wished to the Hennepin County convention. A few delegates here, a few delegates there. It all added up.

The official purpose of the midnight meeting was for the Concerned Democrats to propose their slate of officers for the Hennepin County convention. Their choice for chairman was Vance Opperman. Each of the other nine members of the slate was also a strong McCarthy supporter. Several of them were Opperman's close friends.

When I read about it, I was less angry than embarrassed. I felt that I'd been had. At our ward caucus I had publicly delivered, on Opperman's behalf, a sturdy little speech about how party officers must not be chosen on the basis of faction; that the fight for delegates and the selection of officers were two completely separate matters. Since the officers could have no effect one way or the other on advancing the McCarthy cause, officers should be chosen without regard to that particular fight. Merit alone should be the test. And now the people on whose behalf I'd argued that position had unexpectedly come to power and were proposing an officer slate based on the principle of winner-take-all. Faction was everything; the incumbent county officers, regardless of ability, were to be summarily dismissed. I felt like a chump. I had been used.

And if I was upset by this about-face, what must the average McCarthy supporter have felt! The good men and women who had gone out to church basements and village halls on the first Tuesday in March in order to protest the war had for the most part given no thought at all to dumping county officers. Theirs was a higher concern. If they had been aware of the fact that their votes also affected the party structure, I would guess that they rather casually agreed with the public statements of their leaders: no one wanted to take over the party; the sole purpose was to select peace delegates to Chicago.

But that's not the way the caucus system works. It's not that simple. Just take the case of the elderly lawyer I'd spoken with right after the caucuses. He had brought his family to their caucus, they voted for the peace slate which was handed to them there, and then they all went home, convinced that they had done their share toward selecting national convention delegates who would vote against Lyndon Johnson and the war. And they had. But they'd done more as well, whether they knew it or not. In voting for a slate, they'd voted for a great many names for a large number of positions. Quite apart from delegates to the state convention, they had voted for individuals, most of whom they did not know, to occupy a host of seemingly minor positions: precinct delegate, ward secretary, central committee member, and so on. The sum total of those who hold these various titles makes up what is known as a political party. It's the whole structure. So when the lawyer and his family headed home, proud that they had done their duty, they left behind all sorts of new precinct delegates and party officers. I don't know if the lawyer's family even knew about the precinct delegates and what they were able to do in the aggregate, but the precinct delegates did. They knew that theirs was the power to confer official party endorsement on local candidates for public office. They knew that they were the ones who decided who the higher party officers would be. They knew that it was possible for them to take over the party.

No one knew this better than the group which had just proposed the all-McCarthy slate for the Hennepin County officer posts. Some of them had been aware of the full possibility long before the caucuses. They realized very well where the local power lay.

After it was too late to do much about it, the party regulars began to figure out just what was going on. The first group to sense which way the wind was blowing, those DFL regulars with the most sensitive political antennae, were, of course, the holders of public elected office. Their swift perception is understandable; they were the most immediately affected by the new order of things. The aldermen and legislators and county commissioners suddenly began to think of their own re-endorsement. Their instinct for survival was acute. And so they set out to protect themselves. They began to cultivate Opperman and his crowd.

I was faithful in attending ward club meetings, and I remember one such gathering particularly during this uncertain period. If the Doctor's Wife wanted to use the word "obscene," then she should have seen the frantic obsequiousness of that flock of elected officials trying to move in more closely on the condescending Opperman. They almost mobbed him. Opperman has the most political personality of any man I've ever met, but it has one exception: like many people who talk about themselves a lot, he sometimes lapses into candor. He was often very frank about his plans. *Sotto voce,* he told me, for example, of receiving contributions "to the movement" from incumbent officeholders who were avid, open supporters of the Administration. Of course he took their money. At that same ward club meeting I even saw one County Commissioner hand a hundred-dollar bill (cash was preferred for these transactions) to one of Opperman's lieutenants. All in all, I don't believe I've ever seen so many public officials actually show up at a ward club meeting. Opperman had certainly kept his pledge about rekindling interest in the political process.

Much of his power was still conjectural and depended on his being elected chairman of the Hennepin County DFL. But that was scarcely a problem. Opperman's election was, to put it mildly, in the bag. At least two-thirds of the county delegates were solidly for McCarthy and for whatever slate their side put up.

The extraordinary thing is that Opperman was worried. He certainly was leaving nothing to chance. The energy he applied to his own election was remarkable, especially when you consider that the vote was already sewed up. He was always on the move, promising anything—support, endorsement—in exchange for votes at the county convention. He'd even had a second unlisted telephone line installed. Maybe he thought that many of the new precinct delegates, having made their point about the war, would fail to show up for a county convention that was not part of the national delegate selection process. Whatever his motives, he was working night and day, taking time out only for interviews with the press. He had his whole organization helping him, too, manning the phones and talking to delegates throughout the Hennepin County area.

That those students should at this time have redoubled their efforts is not at all surprising. It was a pivotal period for the peace movement in Minnesota; workers were desperately needed. What I did fail to understand, then or now, is why they were working for Opperman rather than for McCarthy. The date had almost arrived for the rural county conventions, the key to control of all the state. If those same student workers had applied that same frenzied energy to reaching precinct delegates out in the country, rather than in their own captive county, the chances were excellent that they could win twenty-five or so extra delegates to Chicago for Gene McCarthy. The opportunity was there, most invitingly open to them. Doubly open now, since the DFL State Secretary, a strong Administration supporter, had in a moment of conscience, and over the objections of the Chairman, handed over to the McCarthy side all the lists of precinct delegates which until then had been so carefully guarded. The peace movement now had in its possession the names and addresses and phone numbers of all the delegates to the upcoming county conventions. At last they knew whom to reach. All they needed was manpower. Of course one could see that a number of McCarthy supporters were actually working to advance their national cause; dozens of volunteers were traveling all over the state, calling on precinct delegates in Itasca County and Redwood Falls and Lac qui Parle. But the most identifiable element in the peace movement, the West Bank students who had received such a massive share of credit and publicity for the original caucus rout—theirs was a very different story. Those workers were staying at home. They were working a mine which had already been tapped and sealed. They were re-calling names which had been called five times before. At this most critical juncture in the statewide contest, a large share of the manpower available to the McCarthy campaign was consciously diverted to the purely local task of turning a certainty into a landslide. Opperman wanted his margin of victory to be fully as impressive as his press.

That press showed no sign of slacking in its effusiveness. Another glowing account appeared on the inside front page of the Minneapolis *Star*. "Student Rising in DFL, Politics Wins Over Books," it was called. There was a large smiling picture of Opperman over a caption which read simply: "DFL Star Rising Fast." The article contained much biographical data about its subject—Grinnell, Vice-President of the National Student Association, the magnificent caucus strategist—but no mention of his state S.D.S. presidency, though I've since come across that item in the newspaper's own research files. The article quoted its subject extensively on one of the new key issues in his drive for the county chairmanship: money. He was claiming that the incumbent Hennepin County Chairman, Bill Mullin, had shown no flair for fund-raising and that under his stewardship the treasury had become almost bare. These charges drew a response from Mullin, who was quoted a few days later as denying the county's deficit and pleading for a modicum of unity. Mullin stated that since the McCarthy forces had "made their point" in dominating the precinct caucuses, it would "serve no useful purpose of theirs and would only weaken the liberal movement in Hennepin County" to elect a one-faction group of county officers. The incumbent chairman and his eager challenger spent much of the next week debating the actual versus the alleged condition of the Hennepin County DFL budget.

And while all this was going on, the rural conventions grew steadily nearer in time. Not all the early partisans were staying in the cities. There were dozens of activists in both camps who were willing to work for their principles and who saw the state as being up for grabs. They spread out in every direction; some traveled hundreds of miles to talk with a single delegate. It was difficult to be effective without this opportunity for face-to-face persuasion. Even then, the rural delegates were hard to budge. Only a few arguments made any headway. The McCarthy crusaders who carried the word to the hinterland quickly found that the war had provided them with their most reliable text. The Tet offensive had passed from news to fact to history without the Administration changing its stance. People were concerned. If you talked very patiently about the war, it was possible to make conversions. In the closely contested First District, for example, the district treasurer, a hawk before the caucuses, announced that he was shifting his allegiance to McCarthy because the President was simply not moving fast enough to end the war. No one could say how many other original Administration delegates had reached the same conclusion.

On the Administration side, the best argument turned out to be a description of McCarthyite behavior in the cities. The rural delegates place great store in party loyalty. Unlike the urban DFLers, they often find themselves in the political minority; whatever strength the party achieves in the country rests on hard work and discipline and a sense of kinship with every DFLer to be found. To purge is to lose; the rural DFL needs all the workers it can get. So its delegates were particularly susceptible to the horror stories, many of them true, which emanated from the cities. They heard how the victors had carried on as soon as they had won. They heard of arrogance and insult and elitist exclusivity and who could blame them for reflecting that the same might happen in their midst? Rural Minnesota contained much opposition to the war. But its DFL delegates were opposed as well to the unnecessary destruction of a party maintained by their own unceasing efforts; and the only example before them of a local McCarthy victory was one of unbridled intemperance. The war abroad seemed to many to be wrong, but they couldn't accept the need for such a destructive local alternative.

Each side was busy with its strongest proven argument, but there was so little time in which to get it across. Minnesota has eighty-seven counties. There were thousands of precinct delegates. There were never enough workers. In the week before the county conventions, when interest and leverage had reached their peak, all the available individual resources were thrown into an electoral equilibrium which could be tipped by the change of a handful of votes.

The problem seemed to be that not every individual resource *was* available. It is hard to tell how many workers Opperman had deflected from the McCarthy campaign to his own race for the county chairmanship. Whatever their number, they were desperately missed in the frantic fight to win new rural delegates in Minnesota.

They were missed in Wisconsin, too. The Wisconsin presidential primary was scheduled for April 2. Could McCarthy maintain the momentum which he had begun in New Hampshire? As the spotlight glided halfway across the nation, the college volunteers from every state followed quickly in its path. They poured into Wisconsin, the students from New York and Massachusetts and California and Vermont. They came by bus and car and plane. The volunteers from Minnesota had it much easier; they shared a border with the contested state. They could ring Wisconsin doorbells all afternoon without missing a class at the University of Minnesota. They had good Midwestern accents, too, no small concern in door-to-door solicitation. They could be very helpful. And some of them were. But not as many as there might have been. For it seems that the Wisconsin primary came at a most inconvenient time. It would be held only four days before the Hennepin County convention. To some of the Minnesota students, to some of the most experienced organizers, the second event possessed a greater attraction than the first. So they stayed in Hennepin County. They let others work for McCarthy in Wisconsin. With less than a week to go, Paul Newman came over to the main campus at the University of Minnesota and delivered an urgent appeal for more volunteers. He got some, too, many participating in the peace movement for the first time.

Now, of course, the reader may well ask where the author was at this critical point in time. He was in his law office in the Midland Bank Building, Minneapolis, Minnesota, surrounded by Corpus Juris Secundum and his own peculiar brand of tortured doubts. He was helping no one at all. He was dodging the phone calls from one side and becoming rather bitter about the machinations of the other. He was depressed, uncertain, and confused. He didn't mind having to choose, in fact that was precisely what he wished to do, but he was learning that in human affairs the choices are not always perfectly clear.

Sometimes events help clarify things, though. At least, that's what happened to me. That's what had *been* happening to me, I should say, but there are some peaks from which to view the path. My moment of truth, my moment of relative truth, as filtered through a web of caution and weighed upon near-even scales, came on the first weekend of the county conventions, with which it had no real connection. It had to do with another kind of meeting, the candidate-endorsing session of my legislative district.

I live in the Sixth Ward, and I live in the Thirty-eighth Legislative District, too, but, through gerrymander and incompetence, their borders rarely overlap. The Thirty-eighth District has a neighborhood very different from any in the Sixth Ward. It's much wealthier, to start with. Big old houses for the bright young couples who think they're so intrepid for not living in the suburbs. The area is said to have charm, and it does, architecturally. The DFLers in the neighborhood, and some of the Republicans, too, continue to describe themselves as liberals, and even imagine that this is despite, and not because of, their comfortable professional incomes.

Like all the other legislative districts in Minneapolis, the Thirty-eighth is represented in St. Paul by two House members and one state senator. All were Republicans. And in the general election, in November, the two state House seats would both be on the ballot.

It was necessary to endorse two candidates to run against the Republican incumbents. The party constitution required that this be done at a special endorsing convention, composed of delegates from every precinct in the district. These were the same delegates who would attend the Hennepin County convention on the following weekend. I was one of them. I was the sole delegate from my precinct to both events and to several other endorsement conclaves as well. I was discovering an ever-greater network of activity in which the central role was limited to precinct delegates who had been selected almost automatically at their caucuses, the nearly anonymous beneficiaries of straight-slate factional balloting.

(Every day I realized how important those precinct caucuses had been, for they determined the course of the year. Everything that followed them had been set in motion first by all those little neighborhood meetings early in March, meetings open to the public and subject only to majority vote. Everything that was going to follow, flowed from them, too.)

I took my delegate status very seriously. It was the lowest party post that one could hold, but it was comforting to reflect that many of the leaders in the DFL had not made it even that far. And since I was the only delegate our precinct had, I didn't feel that I should miss a single meeting.

So on the morning of the last Saturday in March, I drove over to the endorsing convention. It was being held in a church across from a public tennis court at which the delegates cast longing looks before going in to do their duty. I was surprised at the attendance. The vestry room was nearly filled. Someone was putting up extra folding chairs and I recognized only a few of the faces.

I won't say that I was the only delegate present who wasn't supporting McCarthy; I don't know that for a fact. But I was one of very few who were not wearing the McCarthy button. I looked for an inconspicuous place to sit, and as the room filled up even more I did see someone who I knew had been for the Administration. Bill Wright had been the state Senate candidate from this district two years earlier. He'd worked very hard and had almost won. I had heard that he now planned to run for the House. That seemed to account for his presence; he wasn't wearing a delegate badge so I assumed he hadn't made it through his caucus. I was hoping that he did plan to run again. It was hard to imagine a better candidate. Clean good looks, articulate, still youthful but already an associate professor of history at the University. He would be an even better legislator than a candidate. Today he appeared quite ill at ease. He sat down near the front of the room.

The business before us was very simple. The convention had only one purpose. We were gathered together to endorse two candidates for the state House of Representatives. Endorsement required the vote of 60 percent of those present. That was all there was to it, though endorsement, once achieved, was most significant. Those we endorsed would be the official DFL candidates. The letters "DFL" would follow their names on lawn signs and handouts and sample ballots. But not on the real ballot. The Republicans who control the Minnesota legislature will not permit party labels to appear on the legislative ballot. Even so, the party endorsement carries with it considerable value. In a close race it can make all the difference.

The endorsement of a candidate is in theory the fulcrum of the whole political process, the link between the party and the people. The endorsement is supposed to be a signal. It's a signal to the voters, and it's one they understand. People see it as a kind of code. The party label serves to summarize for them a cluster of facts and opinions which they assume are shared by the candidate as well. When they don't know anything else about the endorsed candidate—which is often the case in local elections—many voters tend to make up their mind on the single fact of party endorsement. This is not an evasion of the issues, but rather a kind of shorthand supplement in the absence of having many facts. The party name itself suggests a host of issues and approaches, to which the voter can be quite decisive in his response.

So when people speak of political power they often are referring to the power to endorse. And they're right, so far as they go. For real power is the power to elect. Insofar as endorsement helps insure election, it remains the central tool of party power. This, of course, depends in turn on how the people view the party at any given time, on whom they deem to be in charge. The endorsement of a political party is only of value when the voters regard that party's leadership structure as being legitimate, when they think the party truly represents its rank-and-file roots. The public's perception in these matters is almost unerringly keen. As we shall see.

For the moment, all we had to do was find and endorse two candidates, though that is not as simple as it sounds. The posts at stake were scarcely presidential in prestige. Legislators in Minnesota do not receive an adequate salary. The problem has less frequently been that of choosing from among a multitude of aspirants for the endorsement than it has of finding anyone to run at all. I wondered whom we could endorse in addition to Bill Wright.

It turned out that there were several hopefuls anxious for the job. I remember two particularly. I don't claim to be an expert on these things, but neither gentleman seemed to be what you might call highly electable. The first was very young, he looked like a high school student though he was enrolled at the University, and despite a rather meek appearance he presented his own candidacy as if it were a non-negotiable demand. Which it sort of was, I guess, since he claimed as sanction for his right to office the full support of that emerging force within the county, the very celebrated Vance Opperman. The young man claimed to be "Vance Opperman's own candidate for the legislature," and the use of this name really did seem to impress some of the delegates. Its effect was somewhat offset, however, during the question period which followed, by the youth's angry refusal to answer a request to state his age. Noticeably miffed, he asked what possible relevance such a question could have. He was informed that state election law did set a minimum age for holding public office. He asked just what that age might be and was told that it was twenty-one. Whereupon he thought for a minute, paused, as if doing some private calculation, and then, smiling for the first time, informed us all that in his case the question of age would not be much of a problem. That's as specific as he ever got.

The other candidate for our endorsement was a good deal more cooperative. He told us all about himself; in fact, he spared no details. It seems that once he'd been a priest. He'd left the Church to get married. He didn't think that this would hurt him at the polls, however. He had brought his wife to the meeting and gallantly bade her to stand up and say hello to the crowd. A little later, when questioned about state issues on which every legislator could be expected to vote, he admitted knowing nothing whatsoever about them. He didn't have to. He was against the war and so he didn't have to talk about this local stuff. That's just what he intended to say as he went about waging his campaign.

I hope my face remained expressionless, but I know my eyes gazed upward toward the vestry roof. Somewhere up there, the pale god of the Republican party was smiling. Where on earth could these candidates have come from? I thought of some of the people I knew who lived within this district—intelligent, educated, committed, able men and women who talked a lot about the issues of the day. I wondered why none of them was willing to run. It was scant consolation to reflect that the previous two speakers would by contrast make Bill Wright look even better than he was. But it was the only comforting thought which came to mind.

And not for long, either. I should have known that things would get much worse. I should have been ready for the next development, but I wasn't. I was taken by surprise when, after someone had placed Bill Wright's name in nomination, a girl in the front row got up and said that Professor Wright was not morally fit to serve. He hadn't supported McCarthy at the time of the precinct caucuses. He must therefore be precluded—throughout his lifetime, was the implication—from holding an office, any office, from dogcatcher on up. She explained that it was nothing personal—just a question of morality.

Wright turned red but said nothing. It was the same with most of his supporters. Almost no one was ready to come to his defense. I recall only one lady who addressed herself properly to the problem—she was the wife of a professor of philosophy and a very early, active member of the McCarthy movement in Minnesota. Her credentials in that regard were impeccable, and so I saw some hope when she got up and delivered a very cogent defense of the gentleman under attack. She pointed out that he was very able. She pointed out that he could be elected. She stressed that he was badly needed in the legislature, since his views on statewide issues had passed every liberal test. She said she couldn't see why the failure to support McCarthy should by itself prevent a highly effective and progressive man from running for local office.

The point seemed simple enough to me, and I refuse to believe that most of the others present didn't agree with it as well. But they said nothing. They just sat stiffly in embarrassed silence while a few young delegates took their time in describing the full extent of the moral degradation of the man who'd dared to ask for their endorsement.

Finally someone tried to take a softer line, but it was already too late. Wright got up and spoke for the first time. He said that under no circumstances would he run. If the judgment of his peers was that his character had now been marked as irretrievably evil, well, then he would of course accept that judgment.

He kept his voice close to a monotone, speaking slowly, deliberately, almost entirely concealing the tremendous effort at self-control. He showed no anger and may, in fact, have felt none. His real emotions were probably by this stage a good deal more complex. The only time he gave a hint of inner irritation was when someone tried, at last, to urge him back into the race. He did not seem much impressed by this tardy expression of aid. He announced that he was leaving and he left. He left the room, and, not long after, he left the district too. He moved out to the suburbs. He's been there ever since and has not sought to run for public office. His departure did not leave us without alternatives for the endorsement. In fact, now we were free to endorse both of them, both the angry adolescent and the smiling defrocked priest.

That did it. As I drove home I was able at least to think things through to the end: I finally knew which side I should be on. I wasn't happy about it, I was anything but ardent, as I edged at last into a soft allegiance of a sort. It was simply a matter of no longer having any other choice.

• • •

I would have called Warren Spannaus, but he happened to call me first, that very evening. He was trying once again to recruit me to work with the rural delegates, and this time I accepted. I accepted even though my teammate on the project was to be none other than Robert Short, with whom my last encounter had been somewhat less than cordial. But that didn't matter any more, at least not to me, the way I'd come to feel.

Our trip was planned for Sunday, the next day, and our target was to be the Becker County convention, scheduled for that afternoon in Detroit Lakes. I knew the area only generally and had to be told that the convention was considered very close. Its job was to elect six delegates to the state convention and our job was to see that all six supported the Administration. It was never made quite clear just how we were to do this. I was told that Short was slated to address the full convention, and I assumed that I was supposed to help with his remarks, since Warren knew that I'd done some speechwriting for Mondale.

We left early the next morning. Warren picked me up and we drove out to the airport, where Short and his new Lear Jet were waiting to depart. I was a little trepidant about seeing Short face-to-face, and he did rather start when I boarded the plane, but after that we both relaxed and got on very well.

No one in Minnesota is neutral on the subject of Bob Short, and I'm in the category of those who like him. He has quite a temper as I already had learned firsthand, but it's no worse than my own and quite transitory. He's intelligent and very much his own man in an age when that alone is grounds for praise.

We couldn't fly directly to Detroit Lakes—the runway wasn't long enough to handle a Lear Jet—so we headed up toward Fargo, where a car had been sent to meet us. Warren Spannaus had joined us for the flight. He was speaking to another county convention that same day, and after we reached Fargo the plane would take him on to Thief River Falls. At the end of the day, we would all fly back together.

Short was in an expansive mood. He denied that he'd ever

berated me in just those words which Warren had repeated, and I told him that it really didn't matter. He explained that he'd been very upset on the morning of that call. The night before he'd suffered a humiliating defeat at his own precinct caucus. Short's elegant mansion is in the suburb of Edina, in a precinct where DFLers are so few that you couldn't blame Short if he expected that only the members of his family were likely to show up. But he told us how he'd arrived at the village hall, at the official hour for the caucus to begin and how at that moment "in rushed a mob of people I'd never even seen before. They dumped me as Precinct Chairman. They didn't even let me be a delegate from my precinct."

Throughout much of the flight he spoke of Gene McCarthy. It seems that McCarthy had phoned Short and asked him to be the treasurer for his California primary campaign. I could readily believe it. Short's energy is legend, and he had in the past served as treasurer for McCarthy's Senate and House campaigns. The two were friends, though Short had not agreed to help in California. He talked about why he thought McCarthy was running for the presidency. In Short's view, McCarthy had never recovered from being passed over for the vice-presidency in 1964. He had been convinced that he would be Lyndon Johnson's running mate.

"I remember the way Gene was talking in Atlantic City," Short explained. "I mean, he was already planning out the whole campaign. I had to ask him, Gene, just why are you so certain that Johnson's going to ask you to be his vice-president? Well, he rattled off a list of names. He had the absolute word from the highest source. Lady Bird had told him he was in. Walter Jenkins had told him. Bill Moyers. Everyone.

"So I asked him: what about Lyndon Johnson? I said, has Johnson *personally* promised you the job? And Gene looked that way he can look, you know, and he just said that he had been given very reasonable assurances for believing he'd be asked.

"You should have seen him when Johnson picked Humphrey. You should have seen that look in his eye. He was absolutely convinced that Johnson had double-crossed him. And now he's busy getting even."

"Had Johnson double-crossed him?" I asked.

"Well, I don't know. You never can tell. I suppose it's possible that Johnson hinted the same thing to a lot of different fellows, just from force of habit. There's no way we'll ever really know. And what difference does it make now anyway?"

That struck me as a very trenchant question.

As we neared the Fargo airport, Short became attentive to the job he was expected to perform in Detroit Lakes. He wasn't sure how to deal with the McCarthy delegates in his prospective audience. He asked me a number of questions about Opperman, of whom he'd been reading so much, and the other students. He wanted to know what they were like and what they were after. I explained that there was considerable variance in their character and goals; different ones were after different things.

Short then launched into an account of how *he* had been a sort of student radical, too. He had tried to run for Congress, when he was younger than this fellow Opperman was now. He had filed against the DFL-endorsed candidate in the primary and by doing so had infuriated the party regulars. Short had been regarded as a maverick ever since. He claimed, with some justification, that the most successful protest movement in recent state history was not this year's McCarthy effort, but rather the 1956 Minnesota Kefauver campaign that he had organized himself. Due in large part to Short's efforts, Kefauver had won an unexpected landslide victory, capturing all the delegates to that year's national convention.

"Now *there* was a rout," said Short, who still recalled with glee how he had shut out all those party leaders who had been supporting Adlai Stevenson—Humphrey, McCarthy, Governor Orville Freeman—and kept them from being national convention delegates. They had been forced to view the 1956 convention from the visitors' gallery. Short's triumph that year had been the result of a grass-roots campaign the theme of which was the repudiation of supposed party bosses. And he pointed out that he was still a maverick; he'd run against the endorsed candidate for lieutenant governor in our state primary just two years earlier. So he didn't see why he shouldn't get along just fine with the new student activists. "Hell," he said, "I'm more anti-establishment than any of them."

The rebel's jet arrived on time, and the car was there as promised. Our driver was a local party man who filled us in as best he could on what to expect at the county convention. He warned that the vote was too close to call. It all depended on who showed up. We were given a rundown of those to whom we should pay particular attention, some friends and some foes. We were warned to be wary of the local spokesman for McCarthy forces, a lawyer most clever and articulate. We were told just who among our own partisans should be given the most credence if we happened to need advice. It was suggested that we take it easy in our efforts at persuasion, since the Becker County delegates desired that their convention remain as decorous as possible. We received the rather pointed reminder that we were no longer in the Twin Cities.

By this time we had reached Detroit Lakes and the elementary school where the convention was being held. It was the rural equivalent of my own Sixth Ward convention at the beginning of the month, and it would today select almost the same number of delegates to the state convention. But somehow this gathering seemed so different from that other. Far fewer people, a much smaller hall, but the difference was even more than one of scale or a sense of orderliness, though that was clearly evident. The real distinction was in the marked absense of strong emotion. I'm not saying that these delegates were *philosophes*; their discussions were certainly no loftier than those anywhere else. It's just that the general approach was one of deliberate reasonableness. Particularly by contrast to the present urban mood, the rural delegates were conducting themselves with a singular lack of passion.

This is not to say that there were not strong divisions. The war was very much the central issue at this meeting. There were the same two sides as in the cities, each concerned with its chances at the county's six state delegate spots. As soon as Short and I walked in we had to huddle with the Administration floor leaders, who even now, with the convention called to order, were having difficulty telling which side had been able to turn out more of its delegates.

The ability to count is perhaps the most important aptitude in politics, and that day I learned by chance a trick that helps in this regard. If you have a political meeting and there are two factions diametrically opposed and you want to know how many are present on each side, then get to the meeting early and help set up the folding chairs. That's all it takes: just be certain that in setting up those chairs you leave an aisle wide enough so that it divides the seats into two distinct sections. When the delegates arrive at the meeting, the members of each faction will sit on their own side of the aisle. They always seem to know who their allies are that day, and they always seem to want to sit together. I learned this tiny truth in Detroit Lakes, as people looked around quite carefully before deciding on which side of the hall they were going to sit. The problem was that after they were seated it still was hard to make a reliable count. Each side appeared to have the same number of delegates. We counted the heads again. It really was too close to call.

Short delivered the first address of the day. It was a pretty good speech, but I'm afraid that he was giving it to the wrong audience. I think that on the plane we'd talked too much about the Sixth Ward students. For that appeared to be the group that now he was trying to win. His remarks were largely a vivid repetition of his own early battles with the bosses in the party. He kept portraying himself as a youthful rebel, too. It's hard to say just how the audience received him in this role. They may have found it credible; Short was one of the youngest men in the room. The average delegate was older than the speaker. It was clearly a middle-aged crowd. But very polite, too, and so when Short proclaimed in basso tones that he was as much of an iconoclast "as any of you young people out there," they listened in silence and gave no sign whatever of bewilderment or surprise. Short finished to courteous applause.

The McCarthy speaker was next, and this was the lawyer about whose effectiveness we'd been warned. I was never able to tell, for no sooner had he started than someone whispered in my ear that I was wanted on the phone, there was a long-distance call. I was afraid that there had been some emergency in my family. No one else knew that I was here or had any reason to call.

I found the phone booth in a corridor just outside the gym and was connected with the party in Minneapolis. It was Bill Mullin. He'd tracked me down on what he claimed was a very important matter.

"Dave," he said slowly, as it was a bad connection, "some of us have been meeting here to plan for the Hennepin County convention next Saturday. You know that I've decided not to seek re-election as chairman, and the consensus here seems to be that you would be a good candidate for the job."

I was reminded of another call from Bill, several painful months in the past, in which he had asked me to run for chairman of the Sixth Ward club and had promised that there'd be no problem at all. This is where I had come in. As I may have noted already, Bill is not discouraged easily.

There was no chance at all that I would accept his offer to run. In fact, the request itself was a most unflattering comment on my own political sagacity; only a fool could have thought that he would win. I assumed that my name was well down on the list of others who had already declined the chance to be the sacrificial lamb. I was not well known in the county, so if they were calling me, they were really desperate.

And with good reason. The most optimistic count made by the Administration side showed that they were hopelessly outnumbered in terms of Hennepin County delegates. Opperman's fervent absorption with obtaining precinct support had insured beyond all doubt his own election as county chairman. His margin was certain to be better than two-to-one.

So it was unnecessary to voice my nagging question, a tactless one in light of Bill's incumbency, of why anybody would *want* to be the county chairman. I merely suggested that the chances of victory were remote.

Bill did not even attempt to deny this, but argued merely that somebody had to run anyway and that I at least had some friends among the students, was able to speak on my feet and might make a more respectable showing than some others he could name. I found his lure entirely resistible, and, of course, I turned it down. For once Bill lapsed from his habitual persistence. He seemed resigned to my refusal, as if he'd somehow heard those words before. After a short pause, he asked whether I knew of anyone else who might be interested in running. I said I couldn't think of anyone. He thanked me and hung up.

I returned to the convention just as the voting was to begin. A short recess had been called during which each side reviewed its strategy. Short called me over to meet in a corner with four or five of the local Administration delegates. It seems they'd just received an offer from the other side. The McCarthy forces wanted to make a deal. They wanted to agree in advance on the county's six state delegates; they were only asking for two and would let us have the other four.

We weren't sure whether we should agree to this arrangement. On the one hand, four votes could be considered a victory from a convention which was capable of going either way. Four votes were better than none. On the other hand, there was the conventional political wisdom about what to do when you're offered such a deal. The savants in the party held to the view that people never offer to take a minority of the delegates unless they've already counted carefully and are sure that they will lose. Six votes are better than four. The decision depended upon an accurate count of the house, but that was still considered too close to be sure. So the local men looked to Short and me to make the decision for them. We had flown out from the cities in a private jet, and we were supposed to know what to do. It was flattering to be at the focus of their quandary, but of course neither Short nor I had the remotest notion of which would be the wiser course. The men who were asking our opinion were the only ones in a position to know what should be done; these delegates were their friends and neighbors. If *they* didn't know about the line-up in their county, Short and I were scarcely in a position to provide some new insight from outside. But that was our attraction. In politics, apparently, any stranger is an expert. People seem to accept advice more readily from them than from those whom they already know.

Short and I excused ourselves—affecting the look of thoughtful concentration—in order to confer between ourselves. We crossed the room to a quiet spot and then asked each other what the hell we ought to advise them to do. I suggested that perhaps we might flip a coin. Short just scratched his head. We had to tell them something, and the convention was being resumed, so we decided to follow the traditional course and assume that the McCarthy offer reflected only inferior strength. We returned to our advisees and shared with them our considered judgment that it was best to go for all six of the delegates. The McCarthy offer was rejected.

The balloting began with the common understanding that the rule of the day was for the winners to take all. This is how it had worked in the city wards, on both sides.

But rural politics follows a different course. There is what may be called the human factor. Slates are presented, just as in the cities, but people are important too. The names on the slates are not anonymous; they represent people whom everyone knows. Some of those people have worked harder than the others for the party over the years. Some have many friends. These considerations can weigh more heavily than one's allegiance to a presidential candidate.

So I never did find out which side had the most people there and I'm really not sure that it mattered. The convention chose six of its best to go to the state convention. Three were for McCarthy and three for the Administration. The fancy plane and the fancy advice of the experts from the city had resulted in obtaining one less vote than if we had stayed at home. It was scant consolation that the McCarthy count had apparently been no better than our own. And it seemed to me that if they could get half the delegation in a place like Becker County, maybe they were going to be able to carry the state. I wished that the McCarthy supporters in the Twin Cities were more like those in Detroit Lakes.

We drove in some embarrassment to Thief River Falls, where the plane and the Party Chairman were waiting for us. If you want to get over a bruise to your ego, try boarding a Lear Jet in Thief River Falls. We were all tired now, and there was less talk than on the way up. We landed at a private field near Minneapolis, and as Warren and I walked to his car, Short called over to remind us to listen to the President's speech.

I had forgotten that Lyndon Johnson was delivering a major address that evening. I assumed that he had invented some new variant of de-escalation to help offset the opposition in the Wisconsin primary next Tuesday. We turned on the radio and listened.

The speech was just what I'd expected until, of course, the end. I wasn't sure I'd heard him correctly, but there was no question that Warren had. He slammed the brakes so suddenly that I slipped off the seat. When I looked up, I saw that his face was in his hands; he wasn't upset, he was just trying very hard to think. Understandably enough. As Party Chairman he was trying to figure out just what was going to happen next. So was I. But neither of us knew.

7

The letters were so big and black, the story monopolized so much of the paper, that of course no one imagined that before the week was out there would be a larger, darker headline still. For the moment, the news was simply that Johnson was out of the race. Everyone had been asked to comment; the columns of explication flowed right to the bottom of the page, seeping well into the inside sections too.

I don't know how the reporters had managed to round up so much commentary between the Sunday night speech and the Monday morning paper, but they had. There were two dominant themes to the printed reaction. The McCarthy leaders were quoted as saying that this development had strengthened their hand. The Administration people, less sure of themselves, were urging Hubert Humphrey to enter the race quickly. There were countless variations on these themes. Everyone seemed to have his say—party leaders from the DFL, the Chairman and Chairwoman, district leaders, the National Committeewoman, members of the Congress, prominent state Republicans, McCarthy leaders, random spokesmen on the street, and even Howie Kaibel, whose viewpoint on the new event was very brief and intrafactional: "McCarthy represents a lot of things that Kennedy cannot represent," he said.

I had my own reaction, too. That onrush of print was proof to me of the pliant responsiveness of our political system. It justified that system; it showed that it could work. The incumbent President of the United States had decided not to run for re-election. Whatever his motives—undoubtedly complex even in his own mind—there can be no question that the insurgency in his party was at the root of his withdrawal. The truly remarkable thing was how limited an effort had been necessary. The public mood against the war may very well have run quite deep, but the McCarthy movement was short in time and small in numbers. However intense its effort or feeling, it represented only a fraction of the total population. Its national inputs were remarkably sparse—some thousands of workers, a few short months, a political alternative which the polls showed to be distinctly a minority view. But the leverage was perfect, swift, and powerful; turn out to the caucuses, turn out of office the most powerful man in the world. It was the textbook case of the textbook tactic, a response so successful in relation to its source that one would hesitate to wish upon us all a system whose hair trigger could be any more delicately poised. How could anyone still dispute the root malleability of events?

And yet the most recurrent cry we hear is that the system doesn't work. Despite an abdication to the contrary, there are those who remain unconvinced about a process which, however massively yielding, does not guarantee them that invariable exactitude which alone can satisfy the fine precision of their hopes. If change cannot be perfect, then the proof of its possibility deserves to be ignored, they feel. I cannot comprehend such a tepid reaction to demonstrated fact.

The fight was still on for control of the state convention. And the outcome was still in doubt. In addition to the national bombshell, the past weekend within Minnesota had seen a spate of county conventions, forty-seven of them, over half of the total to be held. The results had been mixed, and the signs were hard to read even without trying to gauge the effect of Johnson's announcement. The First District remained the most publicized battlefield. Before the weekend, it had been said that the key for McCarthy lay in the Olmsted County convention. If he won those sixteen delegates, the district was his. So now the papers played up what had happened there, a small but sharp disaster of miscalculation.

At the convention, held in Rochester, another one of those local delegate deals had been proposed, this time by the Administration forces. They offered to split the delegation down the middle, each side taking eight state delegates. Eight from Olmsted might still be enough for district control, but the McCarthy people turned it down. I imagine that their reasoning was much the same as that which Short and I had delusively followed in Detroit Lakes. It was a common enough mistake for those who hadn't counted very well. The McCarthy workers were so certain of numerical superiority that they opted for all or nothing and ended up with nothing. Their head count had been seriously in error, a fact that proved far more damaging to their cause than the mere loss of eight delegates, since it served to uplift markedly the morale of the Administration workers elsewhere in the state. It was the first clear sign they'd had that their foe was less than a superorganized juggernaut, unerring as a computer. Perhaps if more of the experienced city organizers had been willing to work outside of Hennepin County, the McCarthy performance would have justified its advance billing. But they hadn't, and so now the word was out that the other side could make mistakes too. The Administration loyalists redoubled their efforts for the upcoming and final weekend of the county contests.

The fight to the finish was apparently just that. We wouldn't know who'd won until the last county convention had adjourned, an event now blessedly proximate in time. The coming weekend would tell the story at last. In the meantime, speculation varied to the most disparate conclusions. The Administration forces had apparently been holding their own, but the McCarthy momentum might still contain some punch. The Minneapolis *Tribune*'s political reporter wrote that despite the loss of Olmsted County, the First District remained "within striking distance" of McCarthy. Perhaps no more than a dozen votes were needed. There had been substantial McCarthy victories in Duluth, as a result of which the Eighth District Chairman, an Administration man, said that he had "no idea" of which way his own district was going to turn.

The key unanswered question was whether Humphrey was a candidate for president. Most Minnesotans assumed that he would be, but the timing was important too. Both sides were well aware of the difference his candidacy could make if announced before the final weekend bout. Twenty years of careful contact with the party would undoubtedly help shake loose a number of delegates from McCarthy in support of the newer favorite son. It could make all the difference. Many on the Administration side felt that if Humphrey didn't announce before Saturday, all would be lost. So they went ahead without him. Humphrey for President committees were being announced in Minnesota towns within hours of Johnson's Sunday speech. Only very tenuously sanctioned by the Humphrey office, they served nonetheless to focus the formations of a cause without a candidate. With or without a formal announcement from Washington, the final round was going to be between two Minnesotans.

One place where this new development could have no effect at all was at the Hennepin County convention, to be held on Saturday. Humphrey was not personally known to many of the new delegates there—which is to say most of the delegates—and his late entrance as a candidate would be largely irrelevant to them. The margin for McCarthy was in any case too great to hazard much erosion. Not that the certainty of triumph had deflected for one moment the activities of the Opperman crew. If anything, the pace of their effort had intensified; and they continued to enjoy the full attention of the press, not an unmixed blessing.

The Minneapolis papers go to every corner of the state. The forces readying for the final assault in, for example, St. Louis County could not fail to read the long accounts of just how absolute the city students were prepared to be. Theirs was the politics of exclusion, with a vengeance. It was winner-take-all in the oldest of traditions, but with the modern glare of unrelieved publicity as well.

The spotlight in those final days was set upon the controversial slate of county officers. Despite the howls of the party regulars, Opperman remained insistent that only the early McCarthy supporters should now be permitted to be county officers. There was to be no deviation from the original Opperman slate. The minority must be completely excluded from consideration.

That minority had some comments of its own. It was requesting some acknowledgment, however token that might be. Bill Mullin and two outgoing district chairmen made public a letter that they'd sent to the Hennepin County delegates. It was a final appeal for inclusion. They wanted a handful of officer posts, not many, just enough to show that their side still remained within the party. They had finally completed a slate of their own—a local labor leader had agreed to run for chairman—but they weren't asking for slate voting. Quite the contrary—they knew they were outnumbered. They asked only that a few from their ranks be permitted to serve. The letter pointed out that in addition to the issues of the war and the presidency, the county organization might perhaps be expected to have a more direct influence in the areas of "civil rights, labor-management relations, poverty, education, housing, metropolitan planning, and all other facets of the liberal program." The letter implied that the election of an all-McCarthy officer slate would be a signal to the others in the party that their cooperation on these projects was no longer desired.

Another Administration spokesman was somewhat more specific and was quoted as remarking that a "reasonable accommodation" would be the election of four Administration candidates out of the total officer complement of ten. He added that if this should fail to occur, it was likely that the assistance of the party regulars and of organized labor would be greatly abated. Whether intended as prediction or threat, his words were entirely ignored. Opperman turned down all efforts at accommodation. The Wisconsin primary, from which he'd absented himself, had been such a success for McCarthy that I suppose he felt that his side was doing well enough now to permit him to disregard anything these angry people said or did. Who needed them, anyway?

So the local complaints about being shut out were never really acted upon; the journalistic sputterings of those last few days remained confined to the papers which were shipped all over the state. The newest Minnesota Poll showed that 65 percent of DFLers approved of Hubert Humphrey, while only 48 percent of them felt the same way about Gene McCarthy. (Robert Kennedy did surprisingly well in this local company, with 57 percent approval.) Few of the activists saw these figures as a harbinger one way or the other; since all the precinct delegates had long since been selected, the will of the party's rank-and-file voters no longer carried much weight at the county convention level. And it was hard to accord much credence to the bullish predictions of either side. With only a few days left to go, there was nothing to do but wait.

The mood was such that even the weather became a subject of political concern. A heavy storm on Thursday morning filled the Humphrey camp with trepidation. Seven inches of fresh new snow and icy roads fast becoming impassable were deemed a sharp advantage to the rural McCarthy forces. As a very general rule of thumb, it could be said of the upcoming county conventions that the McCarthy delegates lived in the larger towns and the Administration people were more prevalent in the outlying farms and villages. It was they who would have to brace the elements in order to reach their conventions. It was just one more factor to be considered, and no one could know when the snow would stop.

No one could guess that the bad times had not yet even begun.

On Thursday evening I was looking through my closet for the boots I'd optimistically put away until next fall. Now I couldn't seem to find them, which was annoying, as I had to go out to a meeting. My ride was due at any moment, and it was a meeting I couldn't miss. For over a year I'd been helping some young black friends to set up a cooperative store in what Minneapolis calls its ghetto area. Our progress had been oppressively slow—this is not the place to recount the limitless frustrations of having to beg for funds from taciturn foundations and the counterfeit committees which the insurance industry publicizes with such incessant cant—but at least we thought we were finally making progress. Tonight's meeting was to prepare the incorporation papers and to coordinate our campaign for the world's most elusive loan.

It was getting late and I abandoned my search for the boots. On the way to the door I passed the television set and saw some letters imposed upon the bottom of the screen. They looked like subtitles. But it was a bulletin: "Martin Luther King . . . Shot in Memphis . . . Stay Tuned for Further Details." There was no sound to the message, just the white block letters moving right to left and off the screen.

I sought to find some hope that Dr. King was merely wounded. Anything more serious would surely have called for an announcer's voice. The program hadn't even been interrupted.

I went down to the street where my ride was waiting. Behind the wheel was a college friend who was serving as the unpaid lawyer for the store, the only other white who had managed to stick with the project. He hadn't heard the news, and I flicked on his car radio. We were setting out for the house where the meeting would be held, a duplex on one of the back streets of a very troubled neighborhood. We had barely gotten underway when the raido reported that Dr. King was dead. Witnesses were saying that the murderer was white.

My friend looked at me. It is painful and embarrassing to report now what we felt. But I've been trying to describe what a certain time was like, and this was very much a part of that time too. The truth is that we felt not only shock and grief and anger: there was undeniably the presence of simple fear as well. It was so ignoble a reaction, I felt so ashamed on recognizing it, but the element of fear was clearly with us in that car. The black reaction to the murder would be understandable enough. It was hard to imagine just what forms it would take. We didn't want to enter those hostile streets tonight. My friend suggested that we call the meeting off. But the girl at whose home we were to meet had no telephone, and so we had no choice. We drove directly to the house.

We parked and locked the car and crossed the dark walk to the porch. A young man standing in the yard next door looked at us as we passed, and if I only imagined that his long hard stare was one of hatred, let that imagining be recorded as belonging to the scene.

We ascended the stairs and joined the meeting, which I was somewhat surprised to find in normal progress. We covered the necessary work in about half an hour, and then we all went into a bedroom and watched the television reports. The news by now had preempted everything else. Already the announcements had begun to speak of riots. After watching for awhile we arranged to meet again next week, and each of us set out for home.

My friend and I walked very quickly to his car. I was angry at myself for being angry at him for taking so much time to find his key. There wasn't much to say during the drive back.

I read the next day that a young white man had been shot and killed a few blocks from where we'd been and at about the same time. I suppose I should have seen that as sort of justifying our fears, but what it did confirm was something else, a much more generalized despair.

From that point on you could perceive a change in the way people were responding to events. The news became consistently surprising, and it was coming in far too fast. A diminished sense of reality was the unavoidable result. For the rest of the year people would get either too excited much too easily, or else not get excited at all. This kind of disconnection would worsen after another murder and a surrealistic convention in Chicago, but the bad signs were already there, and they were bad enough.

There was only one day before our county convention, so suddenly no longer the focus of our attention in light of the national disorder. But the momentum of all those months of planning had perpetuated itself without a hitch; from habit and ambition and all the public motives, too, the busy workers on both sides were preparing for their long-awaited confrontation. The McCarthy side was making one last telephone effort to turn out its majority vote; the mood of the Humphrey delegates had settled down into stolid defiance. They were daring the others to just try and shut them out.

Having learned nothing from my past encounters with this sort of situation, I foolishly forgot to make myself scarce and remained all too close to the phone. The first call on Friday was good for my ego; Congressman Fraser was to give the keynote address on the following morning, and he asked me to help with the preparation of his text. I spent most of the day trying to work up an acceptable outline.

Another call presented more of a problem. A close friend, Margee Thatcher, was the Hennepin County Chairwoman. Unlike Bill Mullin and most of the other incumbent officers, she refused to bow to the inevitable by quietly declining to run for re-election. She knew she'd be defeated by a most decisive margin, but she'd worked very hard throughout her term and as a matter of principle now refused to be dumped without a fight. She said that if they wanted to vote her out, they'd have to do so publicly. She couldn't see why she should spare them the trouble of a vote. She felt that she had earned the right to be returned, and if the delegates didn't agree, they'd just have to throw her out. She was perfectly aware that this would happen.

The purpose of her call was to ask me to deliver her nominating speech. I told her I'd have to think about it and would call her back. She said she understood; I was the fourth person who'd already turned her down. I told her that I wasn't exactly refusing; I really wanted to think about it. She asked me what there was to think about.

A reasonable question. What I was thinking about was having to get along with the local McCarthy majority. I was still close to many of them. If they were to be the wave of the future, very much in charge of the local scene, I suppose I would cut myself out of the picture by publicly opposing them now. It was so easy to argue that hers was a losing cause anyway. Why get up and antagonize the new leadership over a point which was already settled?

But five minutes later I was calling Margee back to tell her that I'd give her speech. I really had no other choice. My conscience is very ordinary, but my memory is painfully acute. I couldn't avoid remembering the time when I had agreed to give Opperman's speech, a perfect mirror reflection of the present awkward moment. I had been angry then that some supposed powers in the party were seeking to intimidate anyone from offering even token support to the students. It seems that now the power had shifted, but the possibility of retribution remained very much the same. Having risked reprisal once, I really had to be consistent, particularly on behalf of a most honorable and decent friend. Margee, to her credit, thanked me for my acquiescence without commenting at all on its delay.

I had dinner with Fraser that evening, and we tried to go over his speech. He wanted to restore a sense of balance in his keynote remarks, but it was hard to think of any phrase that might help toward this end. After dessert we walked back to his office in the Federal Courts Building and tried to get down on paper something close to a final draft.

We worked for an hour or so, and when we finally took a break I called home and found out that a major riot had broken out in Washington. I told Fraser and he looked worried. His family lives near the area where severe rioting was reported. He was anxious for more news, and I went to look for a radio. I thought we were alone in the building, but I saw some light down the hall from under the door of the Marine Recruiting Office, and I was able to borrow their radio. From this we learned of the fires and the shooting which now were so extensive throughout Washington—and very near the Fraser house, judging from the reports. The Congressman decided that he'd better call his wife. I placed the call for him. The operator, who sounded nervous, told me that she was sorry, but no calls could be put through to Washington during the "present emergency." I said that I was placing the call for Congressman Fraser, and she said that made no difference. I put him on the phone to repeat the request, but she told him that it just wasn't possible. We had to hang up. Fraser looked frustrated and tired and concerned. The whole scene seemed so strange to me in that dark and quiet building in downtown Minneapolis—a United States Congressman anxious about the safety of his family and unable even to call them on the phone, unable to do anything but return to the preparation of reasonable words for a crazy convention.

Everything seemed so out of focus and unreal that I didn't feel at all surprised an hour later when a fierce knocking began on Fraser's office window. I went through the lobby to the bolted front door which I unlatched after recognizing a few of the late visitors. They included some of the local black militants who had been most often chosen by the media as spokesmen for their people. They had come to see Fraser, and I took them into his office. They had a list of fourteen demands which they intended to present to the convention tomorrow (tomorrow was almost today) and Fraser listened carefully to what they had to say. I think they wanted his support for their demands, but mostly they wanted him to listen, a very noble practice at which Fraser is superb. I supposed that the keynote speech was as finished as it would ever be, but I arranged to meet Fraser back at the office early in the morning, just before the convention, to go over it one last time. It was past midnight when I got home, and I hated to think of the following day.

That day came soon enough. With coffee and resolve I tried to forget how tired I was and hurried back to Fraser's office. He looked very fresh, though I knew that he had stayed up for hours with his late night visitors. We gave his speech the most cursory look—I can't tell you how irrelevant it seemed —and then we parted; I had to be at the convention early in order to register. I thought for just a moment of my pride a month earlier at having been elected a delegate.

The convention was being held at the Minneapolis Armory, apparently the only place large enough to contain it. I don't know what conclave now claims the record, but I'd like to submit the Hennepin County DFL Convention of 1968 for the title of "Largest Political Convention Ever Held." There were forty-eight hundred delegates, plus the same number of alternates, and at first glance it looked as if not one of them had stayed at home. Thousands of delegates were already in their seats. The balconies which ring the hall were jammed. It was a bigger crowd (and a smaller hall) than at any national party convention. Nothing like it had happened before. In theory, almost the same number of delegates had been sent to our county convention in past years, but in practice many of them had never shown up. In fact, many precincts had formerly failed even to elect delegates in the first place. But this year was different. Lack of interest was clearly not the problem, and so for the first time DFLers saw how truly vast their representation was when all the delegate slots had actually been filled. It was now too late to ask whether a convention this size could possibly conduct its deliberations with even a modicum of either civility or success.

I edged through the throng in search of my delegation and

discovered that the Sixth Ward seats were very choice indeed. Dead center and close to the front, with wide aisles on both sides. It was a well-situated command post, the spot from which Opperman and his friends were busy trying to coordinate the moves of dozens of floor captains everywhere in the hall. These troops were easy to recognize, since each of them was holding a large, new walkie-talkie tightly against his ear. They treated the gadgets with self-conscious reverence, and I could see their value in a room so large, but the picture of those technocratic toys immersed in seventeenth-century ringlets was still mildly unnerving. I saw my friends Katy and Joel and edged my way along the row to the empty seat beside them. From that cramped perch—coats and boots and scarves were piled up everywhere around us—I was able to see every part of the room. There hadn't been space for even all the delegates to be seated on the floor, and high up in the balcony I could make out the printed banners of one delegation or another.

I noticed a number of Humphrey buttons, differing in size and color and in every case the souvenirs of some previous campaign. But if those who wore them were hoping for some miraculous shift in support to their still undeclared candidate, it didn't take them very long to see where the true strength was located that day. A huge majority of the crowd was for McCarthy—there could be no question that they'd all turned out. The room was more like a rally than a convention. Almost everyone had a button, it didn't take much talent to be able to count the crowd. The faces of the Humphrey people reflected hard numerical facts.

The convention must have been in session before most of us were even aware of it. There was no way to hear a gavel through that din. Silence was imposed at last by perhaps the only source which could command it there, a speech of tribute to the memory of Dr. Martin Luther King. The eulogy was given by a black minister from St. Paul, the Reverend Stanley King, a long-time activist in the local civil rights movement. Reverend King is a very accomplished speaker; his measured intonations were doubly effective in their resemblance to the style of the slain leader whose memory they extolled. The message was sharp and effective, and the enormous audience was for once quite perfectly still.

After reviewing the life of the man and the horror of the assassination, the speaker paused for a moment and then proceeded to a further point. He commented on the fact that this was a political convention, and so political remarks might be in order. Whereupon he launched, without warning, into a stirring endorsement of Hubert Humphrey. He produced the litany of Humphrey's twenty-year record on behalf of civil rights and portrayed Humphrey as the only man who now could marshal all the passions which had been so suddenly unleashed.

There was still not a sound anywhere in the room but there didn't have to be. The faces told the story. The audience was absolutely at a loss for what to do. The young people all around me seemed to be in a state of shock; their sense of response was thoroughly confused. They had settled themselves into a state of rapt acceptance of the tone and the content of the eulogy, and then suddenly this almost sacred source had lapsed into the sharpest sort of heresy. He was praising Hubert Humphrey! They were stunned. They couldn't heckle a black speaker. They didn't know what to do.

Some recovered more quickly than others. A motion had been made to send a copy of the eulogy to Mrs. Coretta King in Atlanta. It was a routine procedure, to be perfunctorily approved. But all of a sudden there was an outcry from the floor. Heads turned toward its source, a young man at a microphone who was demanding to be heard. I'd never seen him before, but he was obviously a delegate. Upon being recognized he spoke very forcefully into the mike. His magnified voice was measured but shaky. I can never forget what he had to say.

"I oppose the motion to forward the last speaker's remarks to Mrs. King," he said. "It would be wrong to send her any words which include praise of Hubert Humphrey, particularly before there has been an opportunity to establish just what was the extent of Mr. Humphrey's complicity and participation in the murder of Dr. Martin Luther King."

There was scattered applause from several sections of the hall. I have said that I'll never forget that young man's incredible words, and I won't. But I'll never be able to *believe* the way they were received. They were not only applauded, they were debated. It's true. A floor debate broke out, with speakers on both sides. It occurred to me that Fraser's keynote speech was unlikely to restore a sense of balance to this particular convention. I looked toward the sections where the labor wards were sitting. Reddened faces and incredulous looks. I don't think that what really bothered them was some nut suggesting that Hubert Humphrey had helped to kill Martin Luther King. I imagine they'd come prepared for just such an aberrant outrage. It was the reaction of the audience that angered them. They were shocked that no one else was shocked, that insane remarks were absorbed into the convention as casually as reasonable ones would be. Perhaps it was the size of the convention, plus the fact that every vote was entirely predictable, which permitted such uncritical acceptance of anything at all which might occur. In any event, the debate over whether or not to send the eulogy off to Atlanta was finally resolved when the Reverend Stanley King volunteered to delete his references to Hubert Humphrey. His offer was accepted, and we got back to the business of the day.

That business was the election of county officers. Each person on each slate had to be nominated separately, with separate speeches supporting them as well. Opperman's nominating speech was made by Forrest Harris, the long-time party officer whose early support of McCarthy had so impressed me. Harris is an intelligent man whose dedication to decency has never slackened over the years. I respect him because unlike most educated moderates in politics he never gets discouraged and gives up; after God only knows how many years of caucuses and speeches and conventions and campaigns, his commitment remains undiminished by defeat. I was dismayed that today he was apparently supporting the prevalent mood of winner-take-all. He seemed to endorse the concept of a total McCarthy slate, with everyone else excluded from the party. Since he is regarded as something of an elder statesman, I was hoping that he'd suggest that we choose our officers on the basis of their merit, but he didn't. His remarks about Opperman were close to adulatory. The virtues of the brave young leader and his hardy band were extolled in superlatives which I might have found more palpable without my own experience during the last few difficult months. It occurred to me that Harris hadn't had the chance to work as closely with them as I had. He portrayed Opperman as the brightest star in a whole new firmament. He talked about a new day dawning for the DFL. The applause which followed his encomium resolved forever any doubts about the allegiance of the crowd.

It was strikingly clear now that my nominating speech for Margee Thatcher was going to have a dim reception. At the proper time I went to a floor microphone and placed her name in nomination for re-election as Chairwoman. On my way to the podium, Howie Kaibel grabbed my arm and told me excitedly that I had just disgraced the entire Sixth Ward Club; being tired and nervous, I permitted myself to ask him how that was any longer possible.

When I arrived on the stage and looked out over the hall, I could see that the crowd was even larger than I'd thought. I was very ill at ease with my unpopular duty and consequently grateful that my speech was fully written out. It was the same speech, the same typewritten note cards, which I'd delivered on behalf of Opperman at the Sixth Ward caucus a month earlier. It was the same message, word for word, which Opperman had at that time requested that I give about the need to elect officers without regard to their faction. I began by explaining the similarity of the two speeches, but if I hoped that this allusion might touch the conscience of the majority, I was quickly disappointed. Harris just smiled, and the audience was unimpressed with my attachment to consistency. So I used my three minutes to describe all the successful work my candidate had engaged in on behalf of a number of our party's candidates. I talked about how well she'd done as Chairwoman and asked that she be allowed to continue her efforts in that post. I finished to the depressing sound of scattered token applause.

The minority was small enough, and it was shrinking, too, as the day went on. On my way back down to my delegation I noticed that the labor wards were marked by many empty chairs, more than at the start of the convention. No one likes to stay on throughout a day of preordained defeat, so the gulf between the factions was becoming progressively greater.

My friends in the ward delegation seemed hurt that I had spoken for a candidate not on their faction's slate, but they had no reason to be worried. If anyone was concerned about the outcome, it was me. I knew, of course, what the vote would be, but what bothered me even more was the mood. Some of the speakers were saying the kind of thing for which the angry lunch at the Nicollet Hotel now seemed a dress rehearsal. I saw the president of the state AFL-CIO sitting impassively through a rather pointless but acerbic denunciation of all union members, and I could just imagine what was going through his mind. Throughout the day there was a steady delivery of public denunciation, gratuitous invective of which the only function was apparently to anger and annoy.

The Fraser speech, designed so carefully for its conciliatory effect, was almost unheard by an audience busy talking to itself. The room had become very noisy once again, and speeches were absorbed without effect into the murmurous hubbub of the hall. A moment of relative order was regained for the announcement of our balloting results. As expected, all ten members of the McCarthy slate were elected by large margins—a considerable understatement. Opperman received 3,800 votes, while the labor leader who opposed him ended up with just over 1,100. I tried to console myself with the fact that my nominee for Chairwoman had received a thousand more votes than any of her running mates, but I had to recognize that she had been decisively defeated nonetheless. After the results were in, the exodus of Humphrey backers was accelerated.

This was a shame, because the business of the convention was far from concluded. The election of officers had received most of the attention, but the endorsement of candidates was on the agenda too. That wasn't usually a job for a county convention, but a number of legislative districts had been unable in close contests to muster the 60 percent vote required for endorsement, and so in several cases the responsibility to endorse candidates for the legislature had been kicked upstairs to the present mass assemblage. We all were entitled to vote on each of these endorsements, which covered several different districts. In every case, the post for which we were to find a candidate was already filled by a DFL incumbent. This fact seemed of little consequence to most of the county delegates.

To the Sixth Warders with whom I was sitting, the endorsement contest of greatest interest was that of the Forty-second District. Most of the West Bank students lived there. The incumbent was a man named Jim Adams, who had served for a number of terms. His voting record was respectably liberal, and the reason that the students were opposing him seems to have had little to do with the way he represented them in St. Paul. They weren't so much opposed to Adams as they were anxious to support his rival, a thirty-year old associate professor of history by the name of Alan Spear. Having recently moved to Minnesota from New York, Spear was an ardent McCarthy supporter and, though conventional enough in appearance, employed a radical rhetoric which had endeared him to the students. Opperman's hirsute allies were busy telling their walkie-talkies that Spear was the man to support.

I had never met Spear, but I was skeptical of the prospect of trying to dump a popular incumbent. The DFL had tried to do this to its Governor two years earlier, with catastrophic results. The party had succeeded then in bypassing the incumbent and giving the endorsement to his Lieutenant Governor instead. But Minnesota law provides for a primary election as a check on the endorsement process, and in the 1966 primary, the incumbent Governor had annihilated his endorsed rival by a staggering margin. As a result of all this intraparty fighting, a Republican had won the race for Governor in the fall. I found some rather obvious lessons in all this. The public is quite willing to vote an incumbent out of office, but it questions the legitimacy of a party trying to perform this task in its place.

That conclusion was less clear to many of the county delegates. They seemed to have no second thoughts on the question of incumbency. So when the Adams–Spear vote came up, the majority went for Spear. The Chair was uncertain at first whether the professor had received over 60 percent of the vote, and so we had to stand for a head count. I was one of the few in our delegation who stood for Adams, and I wasn't surprised to see that Opperman was one of the many who remained seated. But when the Spear vote was called for, I was puzzled to observe that Opperman stayed slumped in his seat. He was sitting right behind me, and I turned and asked why he wasn't voting. He grinned. "You know how it is," he said, "I just can't choose between them."

The Chair announced that Spear had been endorsed. Adams looked angry; he was talking to some labor leaders in the back of the hall. He was popular with the workingmen and their families who made up most of his constituency. So was another incumbent legislator from a heavily labor district who lost his endorsement that same day to a botany professor from the University of Minnesota. Labor was not coming out of this convention very well.

Then, we took up the platform. Enough planks had surely been proposed; there were lengthy resolutions on every conceivable subject. Some of these were extremely controversial. I don't know just how much influence a county platform carries in the general scheme of things, but it was precisely the most sensational planks which would be mentioned in the news accounts on the following day. (No paper ever reported the charges against Humphrey, or the fact that they had been rather extensively cheered.)

It was getting late and delegates from both sides were leaving in large numbers for their Saturday night pursuits. The Armory was draining out, though the rough proportions of the majority dominance remained at all times about the same. I finally had to leave, too, though after a long day in the hall a heavy stack of mimeographed resolutions still remained to be officially considered. The number who debated them grew smaller and smaller, and the room as I last saw it seemed a squabbling microcosm of the morning's boisterous throngs. I was discouraged that so little of real value had been produced by a meeting toward which all these months of the most disciplined planning had been directed. But I don't know what else it would have been reasonable to expect.

The Minneapolis Central Labor Union has over 50,000 members, the state AFL-CIO has about 170,000, and there are 35,000 teamsters. And, of course, those members have families. When you add it all up, it comes out to a lot of votes.

To most of the labor leaders, the Hennepin County convention was the place where they had been thrown out of the DFL. This view was not quite accurate. They had been insulted, it is true, reviled publicly and in the most specific terms. Their favorite incumbent legislators had been denied the party's re-endorsement. Dozens of resolutions which they found at best abhorrent had been quickly passed and widely publicized. None of them had been allowed to serve as a county officer, including the incumbent Hennepin County Treasurer, who was also the head of the Central Labor Union, but they had not actually been thrown out of the party. In fact, the new leadership had made it very clear that labor's money was still welcome. It was merely their participation which had been so blatantly denied.

There is a good deal of talk but little knowledge about the financing of political campaigns. I'm not referring to the fund-raising efforts of prominent candidates themselves. A congressman or a senator raises his money through his own extensive contacts, and his contributors have a number of reasons for making their donations. But, in Minnesota at least, and in the DFL, the candidates for lesser office are usually unknown beyond their own small constituencies and find it difficult to raise funds even there. The average large contributor has probably never even heard of these candidates. Perhaps the basic problem is that the more important and more glamorous candidates tend to monopolize the contributor community, and there is almost nothing left over for legislators, mayors, and aldermen. That's why labor is so important. It does care about the local races. It is affected by their outcome. So money is made available for many of these contests, and some of it is channeled through the party. In the past, the Hennepin County DFL could help determine which local candidates deserved the most support. And labor's help was not confined to money. The labor sample ballot was frequently distributed to households that the party itself could not afford to reach. Of course, this assistance is premised on the fact that labor and the party are working closely together, that they support the election of the same candidates.

The incredible thing in the wake of the Hennepin County convention was that the new party leadership still expected the full cooperation of organized labor. They simply assumed that the money would keep on coming in. One of their first acts had been to fire the old county coordinator and replace him with one of their own, the girl whose patient telephoning had helped them carry half the Twelfth Ward. She announced that she expected labor to continue to do its duty. Just what labor envisioned that duty to be was yet to be demonstrated.

For the time being, attention was riveted on the prospects for the state convention. All the county conventions were now completed. Every delegate to the state convention had finally been selected. The Humphrey forces had done slightly better than expected. The DFL State Chairman revealed his own count, which gave 607 delegates to Humphrey, and 512 to McCarthy. If this was accurate, the situation still was less than secure. To control the state convention, 560 votes were needed. Humphrey, still not formally a candidate, had only about 40 votes more than he would need. It was a tenuous margin.

So most of the interest in the contest was focused on the state convention at the end of June, almost two full months away. Everything else was already settled. The effort to win votes was over. The basic fight had run its course in one explosive month. The state convention would only be a final reverberation.

Its results were preordained but unpredictable. They had been set in motion just as finally as all the other recent activity, and if they could not yet be read with equal certainty, it was because of a freakish variable: geography. The state convention was to be held in St. Paul, and most of the McCarthy delegates lived nearby, in the Twin Cities and their suburbs. The Humphrey delegates (whose candidate finally announced at the end of April) were mostly from the rural areas and in some cases would have to drive several hundred miles to attend the state convention. And there was the matter of expenses for the weekend—hotels and restaurants were obligatory for one side but not for the other. One could anticipate that if some delegates chose at the last minute not to attend, it was more likely that they would be from the distant rural areas. This was a constant source of worry to the Humphrey leadership, and it remained the one element of suspense in a struggle otherwise foreseeable.

I found April and May to be very quiet compared to the preceding month. My contact with politics was reduced to reading the accounts of contests in other states—Pennsylvania and Massachusetts, and, of course, with accelerating interest, Indiana and Oregon.

It was a time of respite for me. As one of the large and surprisingly heterogeneous group who found itself in *de facto* exclusion from the party, I was—at times, at least—elated at not being permitted to participate. Aside from some work for the Fraser campaign, I think my total political activity at that time consisted of buying a ticket to a baseball game sponsored by the new Hennepin County DFL organization.

That baseball game was something they really counted on. This was to be the big event which finally got the county office out of debt. It seemed so simple at first. They had arranged to sponsor a baseball game at the Metropolitan Stadium on a Saturday afternoon in June; the Minnesota Twins against the Baltimore Orioles. Tickets were five dollars apiece, with the profits going to the Hennepin County DFL. I didn't know just what share of the take those profits were likely to be—there must have been a charge for the use of the stadium—but I assumed that it was at least a couple of dollars per ticket. I was a little surprised when the newly hired coordinator announced that the county office expected to make ten thousand dollars on the event. That was more than any county fund-raiser had ever brought in before, but with the large new number of political participants it didn't seem entirely out of the question.

The baseball game was the first example of the problem of exclusionary politics. The Hennepin County DFL office had possession of all the past contributor lists. They observed that organized labor had traditionally been the biggest customer for ticket sales. So they sent out letters to every labor local, asking them to buy blocs of seats for the game, or at the very least to try and sell them to their members.

I don't know why anyone was surprised at the outcome, but many people were. The first public news of what was going to happen came in the form of a newspaper story that the chairman of the teamsters had refused to buy any tickets. He had been a delegate to the Hennepin County convention. Other labor leaders shortly followed suit in refusing to give any money to the county DFL. More than forty unions in the Minneapolis area had been contacted, but by the eve of the game only five had chosen to participate. It was announced that the county group expected to raise no more than $2,500, and it was unclear whether this meant profits or receipts. What was very clear was that the sponsors of the game still needed money and that the traditional sources of its procurement were at least temporarily out of bounds.

The paper referred to labor's lack of assistance as an act of retaliation, but I don't think it was that simple. The whole question of contributions had become tied into the matter of electing legislators. When the county convention had endorsed several new candidates in place of DFL incumbents, those new men were entitled to use the words "DFL-Endorsed" on their signs and brochures and sample ballots. But labor makes endorsements, too, and these now went to the incumbents. So in the affected areas there were two competing sets of labels. The voters had to choose between DFL-Endorsed and Labor-Endorsed. The choice did not prove to be all that difficult. Most of the electorate involved in the decision habitually identified with both the groups. But now they weren't so sure. They had read about the goings-on at the county convention, and they had heard more lurid tales from friends. They weren't at all convinced that those now publicly in charge really represented the broad spectrum of the party. It was a question of legitimacy. Getting control of a party's endorsement apparatus is a very different thing from being able to convince the voters of that party that the endorsement reflects their wishes. Very different and much easier. In an open political system such as that in Minnesota, the take-over of a party can be a very easy achievement. It's what happens after that point which causes all the problems. As was becoming most apparent. For the voters of Minneapolis did not so much see their choice as being clearly one between organized labor and the DFL. They tended to feel that the candidates of the former represented the latter as well. They saw the county DFL as temporarily illegitimate. If it *really* were the DFL, they reasoned, it would not have precluded labor men from serving as its officers. They felt that the incumbents were the real DFL candidates. The formal party endorsement had lost its meaning for them.

At the time, I was only vaguely aware of this public reaction. I had returned to my work and had become absorbed in it. Earlier, I had written a book and was now busy revising the galleys. I gave almost no time to politics at all. My disillusionment, or disenfranchisement, or simple despair, or whatever best describes a sense of badly thwarted hope, was steadily extended by events which now I could see only from afar. The death of Robert Kennedy was terrible enough; perhaps the worst thing then was how quickly, almost naturally, people were able to accept the senseless as the norm. There was no absence of grief, but obviously there had been an abatement in the public's capacity for surprise.

• • •

One day I finally left the sidelines and became more enmeshed in local politics than I had previously thought possible, and for a much longer period of time. My decision, such as it was, seems to me very casual in retrospect. The Chairman of the Minnesota Humphrey campaign was a very close friend, State Senator Wendell Anderson. He invited me to come and see him one afternoon, and when I did he asked me to be the state coordinator for the campaign. I told him that I didn't know that much about campaigning, and he argued that it would be a good chance to learn. He said he knew that we'd work well together, which turned out to be the case. I joined the campaign. I hadn't realized until then how much I'd missed the political world of local effort to which my young Sixth Ward friends had introduced me half a year earlier.

So I found myself ensconced in an office with Anderson, his secretary, and the campaign's student organizer, John Haynes, the ablest young man I've ever met. Our quarters were in the same decrepit building where I'd watched the results on the night of the caucuses. It looked like a warehouse with partitions. The building was owned by Bob Short, and it wasn't hard to guess that he had donated it to the campaign; the space was obviously unrentable. There were several large holes in the ceiling. One morning after a heavy rainfall I discovered that my papers had floated into the adjoining office. I kept telling myself that the campaign would soon be over. It was already June.

My work consisted of preparing for the state convention which was only a few weeks off. The basic problem remained the same. Humphrey had the edge in delegates, but it was slight enough to require that all of them show up. The more I examined the delegate lists, the more apparent it became that McCarthy could still take the convention. The problems of geography were fully as acute as had been feared. A number of Humphrey delegates had written or called the office to say they just could not make it to the convention. There were in every case official alternates to take their places, but it was surprising to see how frequently those alternates were on the other side. Some county conventions which had gone solidly for Humphrey had given, as a token gesture toward local unity, all of their alternate positions to supporters of McCarthy. It could be assumed that these alternates were well aware of just which delegates would not be able to make the trip to St. Paul, and so any vacancies would be very quickly filled. Even in those places where both delegates and alternates were for Humphrey, there were indications that the full delegation might not be present.

So the critical job—the only job, really—was to see that all the delegates attended the convention. There were a number of ways to insure the fullest participation, an abundance of urgent reminders and of social inducements to attend. We worked from the delegate lists—long white narrow columns which held typewritten names, one list for each of the eight districts. They came from the DFL office in tight little rolls, and when the rubber band had been removed and the lists unraveled, each one extended almost entirely across the room. In front of every name we placed a letter, either H or M as the case might be. Counting both delegates and alternates, there were over twenty-two hundred names, but I don't recall a dozen cases where the factional allegiance was in doubt. On all those lists we almost never had to pencil in a question mark; it was either H or M and nothing in between. At the McCarthy office, I knew, the same white cylinders were being unrolled and marked with the same certainty of identification. Each side knew the score and concentrated on delivering its players to the field.

It seemed as if we were always sending mailings to the H's. We sent letters from Anderson, telegrams signed by Mondale, and engraved invitations to a reception hosted by Humphrey (these we shipped off to be mailed from Washington with the appropriate postmark). We sent entreaties and directions and reminders every day. If you want to impress your mailman, be a delegate to a close convention.

There really wasn't very much else that one was able to do. The convention was critical; it would select twenty delegates to Chicago and therefore determine whether the Minnesota delegation there was predominantly for Humphrey or McCarthy. This home state allegiance might have considerable effect on the national convention, but all we could do was keep up the steady stream of reminders to our delegates.

Each congressional district had already chosen its five national delegates. In every case it was winner-take-all, and since three districts were for McCarthy and five for Humphrey, it was fifteen to twenty-five in the district delegate count. The twenty at-large delegates could tip the state delegation either way. (One of the five delegates from the Sixth District was Hubert Humphrey, whose home is in Waverly, and one of the five from the Fourth was Gene McCarthy, who maintained an apartment in St. Paul. Our office was surprised at this selection of McCarthy; we had assured his organization that Minnesota's senior Senator would be one of the twenty at-large delegates, regardless of who controlled our state convention. Apparently they didn't trust us and took the safe step of giving him one of the Fourth District spots. That caution, of course, was exercised with the expectation that it would cost them one delegate, since if they had let us send McCarthy to Chicago they would have been able to select someone else to fill the quota from St. Paul. But they refused to rely on our word. One couldn't help but despair of the possibility of ever reaching international accord on any dispute between rival nations when such extravagant suspicion was permitted to exist between two factions of the same political party in a moderate Midwestern state.)

In the last few weeks before our state convention, the key committees began to meet. Each had sixteen members, two from each congressional district, a constant ten likely votes for the Humphrey position against six for the McCarthy camp. The most closely watched committees were Endorsements, which had to put up a slate of twenty names for the national delegate spots, and Resolutions, which, among other things, was expected to produce the majority plank on Vietnam. Equally important, if less publicized, were the Rules and Credentials committees. The question of credentials had become particularly acute. Several county conventions had seen fights too bitter to be resolved, with the result that rival groups of delegates now were asking to be seated. A special committee was trying to arbitrate these fights. If the McCarthy delegations were judged to be in the right, then the margin of victory at the state convention would be even slimmer than reported.

The committees were largely autonomous, and I had no contact with them. I was most familiar with the Platform Committee, for which my brother had drafted the civil liberties plank. Both the McCarthy and Humphrey leaders had accepted his basic proposals, but other draft planks were much less well received. Vietnam, of course, was a matter of frequent dispute. A number of other issues tended to touch off squabbling, too. But there was not nearly as much disagreement as all of this conduct suggests. The interesting thing to me was how very close both sides were on any given issue. On civil rights and ecology and the urban crisis and abortion law reform, there was a very considerable overlap between the views of the two factions. Most of the McCarthy delegates and most of the Humphrey delegates thought very much alike on these matters. They were, after all, members of the same moderate progressive party. On most of the issues of the day they were in relative accord.

But conventions kill a sane approach to issues; the faction is the barrier to ideological *rapprochement.* This was already all too clear in Minnesota. You have a convention, and you have two factions. They are almost equal in delegate strength. Each hopes to prevail. They know that victory depends on discipline. A faction must keep its members together, voting always as a bloc. For if it breaks ranks even once, even on an issue of the widest acceptance, then those ranks might not be closed quite so tightly ever again. Each side becomes afraid to take the chance.

The press doesn't help much either. Even before the convention, while the committees were still just starting to meet, the news coverage served to harden the factional allegiance. If, for example, some Humphrey members of the Platform

Committee joined the McCarthy members in voting for a strong civil rights position, they could expect to see the result reported as a "McCarthyite victory," when it was in fact simply a consensus opinion of the total party. So people who had worked for thirty years to end the nightmare of the black man's fate within this country became unwilling to vote for resolutions which, however expressive of their own convictions, would be proclaimed by the press as a victory for the other faction.

It really didn't matter what the particular issue was. It didn't matter where you drew the line—the other side would be afraid to cross it. It was like a simple game; one side staked out its own position, and there the other stopped. It had very little to do with what those people actually believed. Each issue was defined not by conviction but through the process of political maneuver. A convention is the last place on earth at which the issues can be openly discussed. It's no one's fault; it's in the nature of things.

8 Two days before our state convention I moved into the St. Paul Hilton Hotel. The proceedings would be held in the ornate meeting rooms on the building's lowest levels. In the meantime, there remained much to do. The physical arrangements for a convention can condition its results. Logistics is paramount as the focus of concern. There are all sorts of little things which must be carefully attended to. Like telephones. With several thousand delegates and alternates all herded together in a large and noisy room, communication becomes as difficult as it is essential. The leadership of each faction must be able to convey with great speed its instructions to the delegates. At the

Hennepin County convention, the McCarthy faction had depended on walkie-talkies for this purpose. I considered imitating their tactic at the state convention. But the walls of the St. Paul Hilton proved to be much too thick; you couldn't transmit a message electronically through the air, at least not from outside the ballroom where the delegates were to be gathered. The message just couldn't permeate the walls. Since our headquarters was on the mezzanine, this barrier was most preclusive. We had to depend instead on telephones. In our command post two floors above the convention there was a long table with eight phones. They were the kind of phones which didn't ring—a little bell would be inaudible in the general convention din—but announced themselves instead by a flashing red light where the dial is usually found. Each of the eight telephones was directly connected to its counterpart on the convention floor, one for every district delegation. When you picked up the phone at either end, the other would start flashing. This system did provide instant communication, but it depended on sixteen volunteers each of whom did nothing throughout the convention but sit in front of his assigned telephone, waiting to transmit or receive.

Down the hall from our phone room on the mezzanine there was another room for those in charge of the delegate count. This was the critical operation. During the week before the convention a crew of perhaps a dozen men had spent each evening telephoning every Humphrey delegate and alternate throughout the state. In this way they ascertained just who was planning to attend. They had in every case marked down the hour when each delegate would arrive in St. Paul and the address at which he would be staying. All this information was placed on index cards, one per delegate. It was one man's job to sit with those cards on the Friday afternoon when registration first began and to check off the names of each delegate who registered. By the time the convention started, he would know exactly who was there. Another group was assigned to keep track of who was on the convention floor itself at any given time. Seating was by congressional districts, and within those districts by counties. Someone in each county had the duty of always knowing who was present and who was not. If a Humphrey delegate left his chair to go up to the lobby and buy a paper, someone was supposed to pick up the district phone and report to its watcher upstairs that there was a temporary absence of one vote. This information was passed on to the next room where the delegate count was constantly being revised. So at all times we would know exactly the size of our vote.

The success of this operation depended on the help of dozens of volunteers. We had no trouble whatsoever finding them. Much of the work was tedious, but there was no lack of those who offered their assistance free of charge. There are—I'm sure it's true in every state—a number of people who enjoy that kind of work. Whatever their motives, they look forward to helping out at a convention. This year, their ranks had been appreciably swollen by the exclusionary tactics of the other side. In the Twin Cities there were a great many DFLers who were accustomed to attending their party's biennial convention, but who this year found themselves refused participation. They were not even alternates. The pool of knowledgeable volunteers was therefore atypically large. We put dozens of them to work at the hotel. Some ran the hospitality suite, others manned the phones and worked to keep up the delegate count. Still others stayed up late at night painting placards for the Humphrey floor demonstration. A number of college students volunteered to serve as messenger boys and runners. (A great many of the volunteers on both sides were students; the notion that McCarthy had a monopoly on the young is apocryphal.)

It was to be a weekend convention, Saturday and Sunday only, but by Friday noon the lobby of the Hilton was already full of delegates. The rural people checked in first. The state convention offered them the infrequent chance to see old friends within the party who were from distant corners of the state. Despite the apprehension over which side was going to turn out in greater strength, the mood in the lobby and the crowded corridors was cordial and happy and rather resembled a reunion. I ran into Vance Opperman, whom I hadn't seen for quite some time, and he mentioned that he would maintain a personal headquarters throughout the convention in a suite upstairs: I was led to believe that the suite was a gift from his Republican father.

By late afternoon our counters had reported so many registered rural delegates that I felt our evening reception had been an inspired move. The invitations to the Friday night Humphrey reception had insured that hundreds of delegates would check in well ahead of the Saturday morning gavel. Of course there was another inducement as well. Earlier that evening, before our reception, the DFL was holding a dinner at which both Humphrey and McCarthy would speak. This was being billed as the only confrontation between the two candidates on the same platform at any time during the campaign. So even at thirty dollars per plate, the tickets had been going very well. And a number of members of the national press corps were present to cover both this "debate" and the convention that would follow it. International press corps, I should say; I spent some time trying to describe our county conventions to a British earl representing the *Observer*.

I'd like to be able to relate in detail the exchange between Humphrey and McCarthy, but I never got to see it. I was too busy with last-minute arrangements and the crush of unpleasant detail. There were some very angry delegates to be placated. The Special Credentials Committee had decided to seat the McCarthy delegates in almost every disputed case. The Dakota County Humphrey delegates—twenty-eight desperately needed votes—had requested that at least they be allowed to serve as alternates, a token tribute since all twenty-eight of the McCarthy delegates from Dakota County were sure to appear at the convention. The McCarthy forces refused to concede even the meaningless alternate spots, and the committee backed them up, so there were fifty-six Humphrey people who were furious at our office for not having been able somehow to alter their fate. They were outraged at having ended up with no official status at all. The placebo which we finally found to soothe their sense of loss consisted of a promise to have their pictures taken with Hubert Humphrey. Not a group picture—

separate shots of each with the Vice-President. This seemed to satisfy them, but it certainly entailed a lot of bother. Fifty-six rejected delegates and alternates, plus wives, plus friends, plus some legislative candidates, too, who could just see that picture in the middle of their brochures, all formed a long, impatient line outside the room where we had promised that Humphrey would be found. And he did show up, after the dinner with McCarthy, and posed with evident buoyancy through an interminable series of snapshots. All the while, in an adjoining hall, a large and hot and jam-packed group of invitees were wondering aloud just what the hell had happened to their host. The depletion of our champagne punch did not add to their patience. Humphrey finally made it, though, and whatever else one could rightly say about the reception, it had clearly performed its function of getting the delegates to the hotel safely ahead of time, the night before they were needed.

Ten hours later, when the convention was called to order, they were all in their seats. While the housekeeping business of those morning hours was taking place I moved from phone to phone and tested each in turn. Somewhat to my surprise, they actually worked. There was always a voice on the other end, and it always seemed to be up to date on the facts. I would, for example, saunter over to where the First District was sitting and pick up the receiver. I would ask the man on the line how many of our delegates were seated in the Seventh District, clear across the room. In just a moment, I would have the answer. During that moment, up on the mezzanine, the First District man would lean across the table to his counterpart from the Seventh, who in turn picked up *his* phone and asked the man who was watching its extension on the floor just what the count was at that moment. Since the floor phone-watcher was keeping a continuous count, his answer was immediate. And was relayed at once to me while I still held the First District phone. To check on accuracy, I would go over to the Seventh District and count the delegates for myself. This took some time, but was relatively foolproof, as each of the delegates was wearing a badge which showed his allegiance for either Humphrey or McCarthy. I counted these in every district, and in each of them the phone response proved accurate.

Since I was not a delegate, I had been permitted access to the floor only through a special arrangement between the factions whereby each was entitled to the admission of its floor leaders. That was my title, a most dismaying designation since my personal acquaintance with the delegates was, to put it mildly, minimal. (I did recognize the six from Becker County.) I would have panicked at my own inadequacy for this very pivotal task, were it not for the presence on the floor of two allies who did know what they were doing: State Senate Minority Leader Karl Grittner, our official spokesman for the day, and Tom Kelm, the Second District Chairman. The two men are, respectively, the best parliamentary mind and the most intelligent political strategist of my acquaintance, so their presence was reassuring. My base throughout the convention would be a chair in the front row of the Second District delegation, close both to the podium and to Kelm's invaluable advice.

As I made my way across the floor from one delegation to the next, striving always as best I could to affect a look of informed resolve, I noticed a strange characteristic of many Humphrey delegates. Their lapels and blouses were covered with buttons, shiny campaign-type buttons. In addition to the standard tri-crossed H, there were a multitude of other slogans proudly on display. One of the characteristics of that strange year was the extreme defensiveness of liberals who were not supporting McCarthy. For months now they had been called, to their faces and most regularly, an appalling number of insulting names.

No one likes to be called a Fascist (except, perhaps a Fascist), but the liberals take this kind of treatment worst of all. They develop deep guilt-feelings in exact reverse proportion to the accuracy of the charge. And they'd been hearing for so long that they were venal, rotten warmongers, racists and Nazis, right-wingers and fools that many of these old Stevenson supporters were quite unnerved. They couldn't stand it. They felt keenly the necessity of asserting their liberal convictions. Hence the buttons. I don't think that there was a slogan or a cause anywhere in the liberal panoply which was not being flaunted on some button on some chest. There were Martin Luther King Memorial buttons and fastenings of every size and radiant hue which carried on their glossy fronts a liberal's lexicon of slogans. Every conceivable sort of phrase had been pinned on for all to see: "Make Love, Not War;" "Learn, Baby, Learn;" "Register Guns;" "Aid Biafra." I saw several little buttons whose slogans were puns, and a strange, large one-word stunner which turned out to be Swahili. People wore the things like medals and they thought of them as badges, as passwords to a club in which they wanted to remain.

I went up to the lobby. Some of the Humphrey delegates told me that Forrest Harris had publicly demanded that the convention choose its twenty at-large delegates on the basis of proportional representation, say twelve for Humphrey and eight for McCarthy. I was not unfamiliar with the concept—I knew that proportional representation had been tried extensively in Weimar, Germany—but it seemed to me too late to attempt to implement it now. It was fairly common knowledge that the McCarthy delegates had not raised this point earlier when they still harbored hope of being in the majority, in which case their approach would be very different indeed. They had certainly practiced the winner-take-all technique in selecting national delegates from the congressional districts which they controlled. I saw Harris in the hall and asked him about the inconsistency of his request. He seemed sufficiently embarrassed for me to conclude that his attempt was just *pro forma*. I don't think he ever thought it would be taken seriously in light of what had gone before. Anyway, he seemed more concerned with how the convention would treat the matter of selecting party officers. He was running for re-election as First Vice-Chairman of the DFL. He said he hoped that the voting for officer posts would be free of factional alignment. I couldn't resist reminding him that that had always been my position—as he might recall from the county convention. Then it was my turn to be embarrassed—having pressed too hard an obvious point—and so we quickly parted. I went back to the convention floor.

The morning's business was largely routine. There were the reports of the standing committees, interspersed with a number of obligatory speeches. The Reverend Stanley King gave a very partisan invocation. The Mayor of St. Paul welcomed everyone to his city. Senator McCarthy delivered an impressive address to the delegates, elegant, eloquent, measured, and concise. Hubert Humphrey spoke too, at greater length and not so evenly—there were peaks and plateaus—but often to demonstrative effect. Each man was courteous to the other, and both received standing ovations. There was surprisingly little tension among the delegates at that point, but of course the important voting would not take place until the afternoon. The morning session saw only some voice votes—paper ballots would be employed later for the major business of the meeting. There were only a few warning signs of trouble. McCarthy in his speech had obliquely implied that if his supporters were not given six or seven of the twenty national delegate spots, a failure of the democratic process would be signaled. This view was applauded by his supporters. And then there was a little squabble over just what time the convention should recess for lunch—nothing serious, really, the matter was soon resolved, but it seemed to the Humphrey crowd that what the McCarthy floor leaders were trying to do was delay the pace of the convention. This expanded the anxiety of the rural delegates; they knew that the convention's work must be concluded by Sunday afternoon. That was when they had to leave for home. The McCarthy supporters from the Twin Cities would be able to stay much later. The possibilities were obvious, and unsettling.

But not as unsettling—yet, at least—as the hastily gobbled sandwiches which the delegates consumed while standing during the hectic luncheon break. I took advantage of the recess to go up to the mezzanine and check out all our phones. The volunteers were all in their places, waiting now for the first test of our only means of direct communication. The St. Paul Hilton had provided closed-circuit television coverage of the proceedings, and several sets in our headquarters suite were tuned in to the empty hall. When I saw the convention chairman take his place again at the podium, I hurried back down to the hall.

There was no need to rush, however. The reassembled delegates had quite a wait in store. First they had to sit through several more speeches. Mayor Arthur Naftalin of Minneapolis, in the role of quasi-host, gave his own short greeting—the most intelligent speech of the convention, I thought—and was followed by remarks from Senator Mondale. And then there was a further recitation of the convention's basic rules. The closest possible attention was paid to the procedures governing the nomination and election of national convention delegates. These were heard in attentive silence and followed by a number of questions from the floor. There was no real disagreement on the rules, but quite a bit of caution. The moment of truth was almost at hand.

It was after four o'clock when all the rules had finally been discussed and clarified. But even then it was not time for the convention to move on to the election of its national convention delegates. There was a challenge from the floor which had to be settled first, a challenge to the seating of the delegation from Carver County. This was one of the four county conventions—the much-photographed Dakota County being another—the outcomes of which had been in real dispute, so much so that a bifactional committee had been appointed to determine whether the McCarthy or the Humphrey side deserved to be seated in each case. Two of the three members of this committee were Humphrey supporters, but in three of the four cases they seated the McCarthy delegates. The exception had been Carver County with six state delegates. The decision of the committee with regard to Carver County now had to be put to a vote of the convention.

Some of the Humphrey delegates were annoyed by this delay. The committee's findings had already cost them many valuable votes, but they had accepted them without a challenge, a challenge which would likely have prevailed on that convention floor if pursued on purely factional lines. It seemed to them unfair to force just such a vote now on the one small disputed county whose cause had been studied and adjudicated in the same fashion as the others. But mostly, though, their concern was with the delay this vote would cause. Delay was the only danger which the Humphrey delegates feared. Delay, if prolonged enough, might last until they had to leave; it could cost them their majority. They saw this McCarthy challenge as tactic, not principle, and resented the move to outwait the effectiveness of their own legitimate franchise.

The minority case for Carver County was presented at considerable length. Several delegates delivered lengthy arguments. There were speeches for each side. Members of the arbitration committee explained their basis for seating the Humphrey delegates. After quite some time the matter was put to a vote —the voice vote which had been standard up until then. The Chair ruled that the committee's decision had been affirmed; the six Humphrey delegates could take their seats at this convention. The ruling was immediately challenged from the floor. The McCarthy floor leader called for a roll call vote—for the use of paper ballots, so that the results could be precisely known. That didn't seem to me an unreasonable request; it would eliminate any question of the Chair's having heard the vote correctly. But I was concerned with the problem of time. It was already very late in the afternoon. The debate on the Carver County matter had seemed interminable. And the process of the paper balloting would now consume even more time. Our rules provided for paper ballots whenever requested by one hundred of the delegates; so either side could easily pursue this course whenever it so wished. The McCarthy side so wished. Instructions were given by the Chair to pass out the ballots to the delegates.

Even after everyone had had a chance to vote on the Carver County problem, there was still the job of counting the ballots. This was assigned to a bifactional team of tellers. It would take them almost an hour.

In the meantime, the convention had finally arrived at the matter of the national convention delegates. The Chairman of the Nominations Committee came up to the podium and read the twenty names of the Majority Report. The room was very still. Most of the crowd was hearing this list for the first time. The Nominations Committee itself had not been able to agree on twenty names until the last minute. The problem was very simple; there were not enough places to go around. One can think of a number of "natural" delegates who usually represent their state at a national convention—senators, congressmen, top party officers, mayors of large cities, those party workers who have toiled to most effect. These are rather obvious choices, as can be seen by looking at past convention lists. But most of them lived in the Twin Cities area. In other years, they would have been national delegates from their own congressional delegations. In 1968, however, those positions had been filled with McCarthy supporters. Many of them were new to politics —Howie Kaibel, for example, was one of the five national delegates from my district—and while the infusion of new names is a very good thing in itself, it did raise the problem of what to do with the old ones. With some of these, the Nominations Committee really had no choice. They couldn't turn down Senator Mondale, or Congressman Fraser or Congressman Karth, or the Party Chairman and Chairwoman. They had permitted the convention's Black Caucus to add one name of its own to their twenty-man list. Since none of the national McCarthy delegates was identified with organized labor, the committee also had been sure to select the presidents of the State AFL-CIO and of the Teamsters. Then there was the only DFLer who held state-wide executive office, Minnesota's Secretary of State. He had to be included, as did Orville Freeman, the Secretary of Agriculture and a former governor of Minnesota. This did not leave many empty places on the twenty-member list. And there were so many people who wanted to be chosen. Most of the obligatory choices of the Majority Report resided in the Twin Cities; the rural Humphrey delegates were demanding their fair share of the twenty at-large positions too. So the Nominations Committee had been forced to reject at least two aspirants for every one they chose. Like all successful compromises, this left no one fully satisfied. Except, perhaps, the twenty who had made it on the list. The nomination of some of them, like Mondale and Fraser, met with widespread approval. Others, like Bob Short, elicited a much more mixed response.

Now it was time for the Minority Report, prepared by the McCarthy members of the Nominations Committee. Since it looked to them as if they didn't have the votes to push through twenty names of their own, they were relying on another strategy. To start with, they didn't even try to put up twenty names. They put up only ten. That gave the appearance of a conciliatory approach—they weren't asking for all the delegates, just for some of them. This move had another advantage too, potentially far more useful. It was thought that not every Humphrey delegate could support enthusiastically every name on the Majority slate; there might well be some defections. Perhaps fifty or sixty or even more of the Humphrey people would pass up a few of the Majority nominations and substitute instead a few from the Minority slate. If that happened, it was imperative that these votes not be diluted across a galaxy of names. If the aberrant Humphrey votes were directed to a narrow choice of McCarthy names, then perhaps some of those names might get enough votes to make it. It was a complicated little strategy, but the possibility existed that it might actually work.

Another part of the McCarthy plan was easier to follow. The ten McCarthy names included the mayors of Minneapolis and St. Paul, both of whom were well-known Humphrey supporters. The tense suburban lady who placed their names in nomination charged that it was "disgraceful" that neither had been listed on the Majority slate. I was one who wished that they'd been put there, too, but I had no illusions as to why they were being placed on the McCarthy list of nominees. Their presence there would make it that much easier for urban Humphrey supporters to cross over from their own slate, at least in those two cases. And when such switching starts, it may become contagious. One of the McCarthy floor leaders told me that the whole idea was to chisel a crack in the dike of Humphrey discipline. I could believe it. It was very clear that the mayors were being used; their inclusion on the

McCarthy slate surely had nothing to do with principle. I recalled that neither mayor had been permitted to be even a precinct delegate by the McCarthy forces who controlled their cities back in March. This new-found concern for their delegate status seemed somewhat tardy at best. As convention strategy, though, it was resourceful, I had to admit.

But strategy depends on discipline. And on communication, too. You have to let your people know just what they're expected to do. The planning which produced the careful Minority slate had not been shared with all the McCarthy delegates on the floor. Or even with all their leaders, some of whom began to nominate "McCarthy"—as opposed to "Minority"—delegates of their own. The list grew very quickly. Before long there were more than twenty McCarthy candidates in nomination. This was inconsistent with—it would be absolutely fatal to—the basic McCarthy plan. More than twenty names would guarantee disaster. There were hasty, whispered huddlings on the floor between spokesmen of the various subfactions of the McCarthy cause, and then, a few minutes later, after the strategy had finally been explained, many of the recent nominees arose in turn to ask that their names be withdrawn from consideration. Of course this took up still more time.

While all of this was going on, I had to participate in a basic decision of strategy too. The question for the Humphrey forces was whether or not to call for a recess. The problem was that it was almost time to vote for national delegates. Well and good. But traditional convention wisdom dictates that one should never proceed to the major vote without having had some sort of test vote first. The most significant decision which had brought us to St. Paul was the election of twenty national delegates. All twenty would be elected by one ballot, and it was absurd to have that ballot cast without knowing in advance just what was the division of the delegates on the floor. The best way to know this was to take another vote first, on another matter. (Assuming, as one could at that convention, that all voting would be along the same tight factional lines.) And in fact there had already been such a vote—the vote on the seating of the Carver County delegates. The trouble was that the results of that ballot were still being counted. We didn't know what they would be. The totals would probably be announced just before the balloting on delegates, but by then —if the first vote was declared to be a victory for McCarthy— the move for a recess would fail. The McCarthy delegates, finding themselves in the majority, would defeat it and rush right on to the delegate vote. Caution suggested, therefore, to the worried Humphrey strategists that a recess should be called. It would probably pass; it was time for a dinner break anyway. During the recess, the first vote totals would be made available, and if these showed a McCarthy win, there would still be time to try and round up the missing Humphrey delegates before we reconvened. But that raised still another hazard: the basic problem of time. The recess and dinner would use up several precious hours. Our greatest danger remained the departure of the rural delegates on the following afternoon. We had to conclude the convention's business before that point was reached. Each hour was precious. We really couldn't afford the luxury of a recess, but we had to know with some precision how the first vote would turn out. It seemed impossible to satisfy both needs.

There was only one thing to do: rely solely on our telephone count. If our communications network was as accurate as we had planned, it could provide us with the information that we needed. It could tell us whether or not we really needed the recess. If it was accurate, that is. We had to take it on faith and that is exactly what we did.

I picked up the Second District phone and asked the man on the other end to give us his latest count. I held on while he had his co-workers phone to each of their districts and then check the results against their card files. In about three minutes he reported back his answer: the Humphrey forces were in the majority. There was no need to recess. According to him, when the first ballot had been taken there were 1,110 delegates on the floor. His running tally showed that 622 of them were Humphrey delegates, 488 were for McCarthy, with just one vote uncertain.

I went over to the little group of Humphrey strategists—Anderson, Kelm, Grittner, and one or two others. I gave them the count from upstairs. If it was right, we should proceed right away with the vote on the delegates. If it was wrong . . . I didn't even like to think about that. One of the group, tired and nervous, asked me whether we could really rely on the telephone count. I said that I was sure we could. He gave me a look which conveyed very well the personal consequences should my answer not be justified. We concluded that we'd go ahead; we'd risk a vote without a recess.

I confess that I was ill at ease. It seemed forever before the first vote totals had finally been counted. They were read to the crowd just before the delegate ballot was about to be taken. Everyone listened anxiously, no one more so than I.

As if to prolong the agony, the results were announced by congressional district. You couldn't get the total until the very end. And there it was: for the Humphrey side on the Carver County question, 623 votes; for McCarthy, 487. Our system of counting had worked. We had only been one vote off. For the first time in several months we could stop worrying about how many of our delegates would show up.

It was time to vote for the national delegates. I saw the tellers bring the fresh new ballots to the podium. The freshly printed sheets of paper were distributed throughout the room. Since my side was clearly in the majority now, I was able to observe the balloting with the dispassion of a spectator. I could relax.

But then something happened. Something unexpected, something stupid, a mistake. At first I couldn't believe it. A delegate from Rice County asked to be recognized from the floor. She stood at a microphone with her ballot in her hand. She was holding it high in the air. She announced that one candidate's name was missing from the ballot.

For just a moment all one heard was a busy rustling as each delegate checked through his own ballot to see if this was true. It was. The name of a lady who had been nominated from the floor had been somehow overlooked by the typist who prepared the stencils for the voting.

The response to the error was predictable. Now it was the McCarthy side which saw the desirability of a recess. One McCarthy spokesman moved that new ballots be run off to rectify the omission. This would take about an hour. It was now past 6:00 p.m. It was the normal time for dinner. There would have to be a recess.

One delegate did suggest that things would move a lot faster if everyone simply penciled in the single missing name. But no, the Chair (a Humphrey man) ruled that new ballots must be printed. This was greeted with wild applause from the McCarthy delegates, one of whom then moved to recess without delay. A spokesman for the Humphrey side got up to comment on the motion. He asked that everyone vote for it. It was the reasonable thing to do. And of course the Humphrey delegates were hungry, too; some of them might vote for a chance to eat. Perhaps their spokesman feared a public break in the factional ranks, even on a matter such as this. With his support, in any event, the motion clearly carried.

So there we were, the strategists, alone in an empty hall. Everyone else had rushed right off to dinner. All the maneuvering on the part of each side, and it was a typist's error which had finally determined what took place. Despite the near-perfection of our continual telephone count, we'd ended up with a recess after all.

Only now the problems of that pause seemed all the more acute. Just a few minutes earlier we'd had a clear majority of the delegates. Now we had to get them back. I discovered with a sinking heart that many of them were scattering throughout the downtown St. Paul area—the Hilton's restaurants could hold only a fraction of the delegates.

I went up to our headquarters and was relieved to find there that a number of our student volunteers were still waiting around to help. I sent them out in pairs to the restaurants and bars which were close to the hotel. I told them to phone headquarters every fifteen minutes from wherever they might be. Then I watched the closed-circuit picture of the convention hall until I saw it start to fill up again, about an hour later. I told our staff that when the student volunteers called in they should be instructed to go up to every diner wearing a Humphrey delegate badge and tell them to hurry back to the Hilton. We were about to go back into session.

When I got down to the floor myself, things were already underway. The very first order of business was the election of the national delegates. I saw the paper ballots being carried in again, but this time I saw them with considerably more concern. I couldn't help but wonder how many delegates were still lingering over dessert. I picked up the floor phone as if it were a talisman and waited very nervously to learn the latest count. The answer came less quickly than before. The upstairs room apparently was a madhouse; it was becoming very hard to keep track of our nomadic delegation. Finally I was given the report: our margin was at least as good as it had been before. Our delegates were now back in their seats. I hoped so, for even as I passed this message on to our floor leaders the delegates were in the process of marking their ballots. The selection of national delegates was finally taking place.

The ballots were collected and then taken by the tellers to a room just off the hall. It would take about an hour to tabulate the results. A very long hour. The convention used this time to consider other business. There were nominating speeches for a variety of party posts: for state chairman, for national committeeman, for national committeewoman, for the party's chairwoman, a post which was being vacated. In all four cases the McCarthy delegates nominated their own candidates, and in the first three they were challenging incumbents, a procedure entirely proper in itself—that's why there are conventions. But as the nominating and seconding speeches were heard for each of the contested posts, I was disturbed at a tone which was becoming increasingly harsh. During the day, the McCarthy speakers had resorted to reason, facts, and, on occasion, eloquence in advocating their cause. There was never a deviation from this courteous approach. But, of course, at that time it was possible for them to think that they had a majority of the votes. Then the Carver County balloting had shown the true state of affairs. And so now their speeches were of a different sort—angrier, vituperative. Reason was displaced by sheer invective. Their speeches and, consequently, the mood of the entire convention, grew steadily more ugly as the evening session went on.

What disturbed me most was their target, not their tone. Speaker after speaker castigated not some nominee for delegate, not Hubert Humphrey either, and not even the war very much; instead, they concentrated their attacks on the political process which had led to this convention and the procedures of its operation. Without much explanation, but with escalating scorn, they reviled the political process in the harshest possible terms. They spoke of a "denial of the democratic process," of "corrupt leadership," of the absolute frustration of the proven majority view.

I am not wholly unfamiliar with what goes on in other states. There are all too many places in this country where the democratic process really is denied. I know that there are states where the national convention delegates are selected by a handful of party bosses quite oblivious to the wishes of the average voter.

But this is not the case in Minnesota. My defense of this point is prompted not by chauvinism, but by acquaintance with the facts. The political process in our state has not yet reached perfection, but in Minnesota it is true that the process is entirely open. Except in the most local sense, there is no such thing as a party boss. In 1966, both our Senators, Mondale and McCarthy, announced to a state DFL convention their support of the incumbent governor—and not one vote was changed; the convention went on to endorse another man. The basic fact of political life in Minnesota is that power and influence flow upward from the precinct caucuses, and those caucuses are open to the public. Everyone is eligible to attend. And in 1968, many people did. They all had the same chance to vote for ward and county delegates, who in turn gathered later on to choose representatives to the state convention. Now those representatives were gathered in St. Paul. And more of them were for Humphrey than for McCarthy. This was not a denial of the mood within the state—it was rather its reflection. And any distortions in that mirror tended to favor McCarthy. About 55 percent of the state delegates were for Humphrey, with 45 percent against. Every poll taken within the state showed that Humphrey's lead with DFLers was a good deal larger than that at the convention. The McCarthy cause, if anything, was over-represented there. So it was frustrating to hear the sins of other states described as if they were home grown.

One point that the speakers made was valid on its face. They were asking why, since they had over 40 percent of the state delegates, they should not be given 40 percent of the national delegates too. Why not indeed. A good question, with a somewhat ironic answer: the practice of winner-take-all had been set in motion by the McCarthy movement itself and could not fairly be reversed at a point well past midstream. In my own congressional district convention, for example, about 40 percent of the delegates had been for Hubert Humphrey, but all five of those chosen to go to Chicago had been solid McCarthy supporters. There was no way to change that now, and so one would have thought that the case for proportional representation had been laid to rest by those who now were trying to exhume it. In fact, the McCarthy leadership had never raised the issue of proportional representation until that moment at the state convention when they knew they were in the minority. It must therefore be assumed that they had come prepared to take all twenty at-large delegates for themselves if only they could muster the votes.

Both sides had been preparing for the state convention for months. There had been endless conferences between the camps, interminable statements by each to the press. If one side had genuinely sought to apportion the delegates between the two camps, it would surely have announced this plan before the convention began. There was indeed, to quote from one of the angry speeches, a rather significant credibility gap.

(It is interesting to see what happened once the issue *was* finally raised. The 1968 DFL convention voted overwhelmingly to appoint a commission to reform the party's constitution. That commission's recommendations were adopted by the party a year later, and so the DFL now requires that its national convention delegates be selected according to a plan of proportional representation.)

The speeches seemed to go on forever and did in fact fill several hours with alternating oratory on behalf of first one faction's candidate, then his rival. Each party office was taken up in turn, equal time allotted for all in a steady series of opposing remarks, an unbroken pattern of paired contention. One speaker intoned his candidate's past service to the party, and then was followed, as if in rebuttal, by the advocate for the challenger, with sharp remarks disparaging the entire process. In the meantime, the national delegate votes were still being counted in the small room off the hall. It was after eleven o'clock before the tellers had finished their work. The silence was total as we listened to the list of winners, the twenty names we would be sending to Chicago. It was the Humphrey slate, without exception. The votes were bunched together, there had not been much of a spread. Congressman Fraser had received the highest total, 664 votes, while Bob Short, the lowest of the winners, had 613. The highest count for a McCarthy nominee was 468. The results were similar to the totals on the first vote of the day. The early break for dinner had caused no erosion in the numbers committed to either side. The gap between the factions was much the same as before.

So the votes which remained to be taken—that night, at least—were no longer subject to the slightest doubt. The certainty now of the numerical outcome reinforced each side in its particular approach. The Humphrey delegates pushed for, and won, the right to hurry up and ballot for the twenty alternate positions and for the four contested party posts. The McCarthy side, for its part, concerned itself with intensified invective. A professor of philosophy quoted from an old speech of Humphrey's, in which members of the Communist Party were described as having "no part in determining its goals and are not permitted to voice dissent to party objectives"; the professor said that this described the DFL as well. As the abuse continued, so did the balloting. It was now very late, and when the attempt was made to begin consideration of the platform and resolutions, a McCarthy floor leader moved that those matters be put off until the next day. The motion was carried by a heavy margin. It was almost midnight, and both sides had yet to caucus and plan their strategy for Sunday. So the convention voted itself into recess until ten-thirty on the following morning. The delegates left the hall without knowing the results of the last balloting, which would have to be tabulated during the night.

I wanted to get some sleep, but instead I went upstairs with Anderson, Kelm, and the others to talk about our plans for the day which had just begun. Considering the way the balloting had gone on Saturday, we ought to have been jubilant, but the mood of our tired little group was one of trepidant concern. There was so much left to cover during the Sunday session. In addition to electing the other party officers, there was the platform to be considered and all of the resolutions. Whatever else might be rushed through, we felt it was imperative that the platform planks on Vietnam and human rights receive the most extensive debate. The former subject in particular was the cause of the split in the party. It would be a mockery of that party, of the very concept of a viable political institution, to gloss over or restrict discussion of the issue which had permeated every aspect of the year. And human rights, though not a matter of factional dispute, deserved the same careful deliberation. Regardless of the press of time, to give limited attention to either of these concerns would be to justify the worst charges that had been made about the repressiveness of our system.

We were all agreed on this. Those two planks had to be the focus of the day. With that fact assumed, we moved on to an old problem now distressingly imminent—the departure of our delegates. The convention was set to reconvene at ten-thirty on Sunday morning. By five or six that afternoon—at the very latest—many of our delegates would be leaving the hotel. They had to be at work on Monday morning, in many different parts of the state. It was imperative that our business be concluded before they started to leave. For if their departure did take place, the McCarthy delegates would find themselves suddenly in the majority. It would then be possible for them to call for a new vote on everything which had already been decided by the full convention. They could throw out the twenty national delegates and elect twenty new ones of their own. Perhaps it was unfair of us to even speculate on this as possible; such a last-minute ploy on the part of the remaining delegates would have been a direct repudiation of all the recent talk about responsiveness and fair play. To suspect the McCarthy delegates of contemplating such a move was scarcely very flattering to them. But I've never tried to suggest that the paranoia of that year was limited to only one side in the struggle.

Still, we didn't think we really had a problem. We looked at the agenda and found its brevity reassuring. We saw that there was time enough. One brief ballot at the start of the Sunday session would settle the remaining officer posts, and after that the entire day could be devoted to debate on the platform. Everyone would have a chance to participate in the discussion, and we could still adjourn in time to avoid reversal by a trick. Or so it seemed at that late hour.

9 The Sunday session started almost on time, which I took as a happy portent for the outcome of the day. Our delegates looked much the worse for wear, whether from the marathon session on Saturday or the celebrations which had followed it, but all of them seemed to have made it back to their seats for the final session. Our telephone count confirmed this, and it was fairly obvious, too, from just a glance around the room that we had the same full house as the day before.

Which meant the same division of the vote, and, as if we

needed a reminder of what that vote had been, the day began with a recitation of the results from the night before. The Humphrey candidates had prevailed in every case—the alternate delegates, the top party officers, the national committee posts. The margin of victory had held, had even grown a little.

The Chair announced that as soon as the other officer posts could be filled we would move right on to the two key platform planks. I looked at my watch and was glad to see that we were slightly ahead of schedule.

The Chairman of the Nominating Committee came up to the podium with his list of nominees, to which other names could be added from the floor. He began with the position of first vice-chairman, the highest unpaid officer post in the party. At the mention of this job the crowd became attentive. This was, one thought, the last moment of suspense that the convention would have, for the incumbent First Vice-Chairman was Forrest Harris, the only McCarthy supporter who was seeking return to a high party post. The Nominating Committee was dominated by Humphrey supporters, as was, of course, the convention itself. It would have been very easy to replace Harris with a Humphrey man.

Since this was precisely the sort of tactic in which Harris himself had participated on those earlier occasions when he had the votes, he was in no position now to criticize the delegates, should they decide to let him go. It was a question of precedent. But the precedent was not followed. The name of Forrest Harris was read off as the committee's nominee for the post.

I looked at Harris and he looked nervous. To be the choice of the Nominating Committee is all very well, but it's no guarantee of success. The committee, after all, is only making a recommendation, which delegates have often disregarded in the past. Harris wasn't the only one who looked nervous. Many of the McCarthy delegates were apprehensive about his chances. The official endorsement was to them no solace; just the opposite in fact—if the Humphrey-controlled committee had come out for Harris, there had to be some trick involved. The committee move must be for the sake of appearance alone. Just wait and see, some challenger would soon be nominated from the floor.

But further nominations were already being called for, and there was absolutely no response. After several moments of sanctioning silence, it was moved that Harris be unanimously elected. The motion carried with no opposing votes.

There was some scattered applause among the McCarthy delegates, a number of whom were congratulating the victor. I was mildly annoyed at their exuberance. What had they expected from their opponents? At our planning sessions we'd never even considered dumping Harris from his party post. These words are self-congratulatory and rather smug as well, but the fact is that the Humphrey supporters in Minnesota had from the outset been concerned primarily with winning delegates and not with purging officers. That practice had been the prerogative of the other side, whose members now seemed astonished that their example was not being followed.

They did manage to recover, though, in time to offer nominations of their own in opposition to some of the other incumbent candidates for the state officer positions. Now that the one McCarthy incumbent had been safely re-elected, there was no risk to them in these later challenges—one of which actually succeeded. The McCarthy candidate for party secretary defeated the incumbent, a strong Humphrey man. That he was able to do so only with the support of several hundred Humphrey delegates did not serve to restrain the cheers of triumph with which his victory was greeted by his faction.

It was past noon before all the nominating speeches and the balloting for officers had been completed. I couldn't help but wish that there had been fewer of those orations and that they'd taken up less time. Soon we'd have to break for lunch, and we still hadn't begun discussion of the platform. I'd been hoping that we could be into that by the middle of the morning session. Now it seemed that the afternoon alone was going to have to suffice. That was bad enough, and of course, there remained the other problem, the need to finish up before our delegates went home. That was a persistent worry, a constant threat which made each minute freeze in time. The fulsome little nominating speeches had seemed interminable. I was surprised at how relieved I felt when they were over. I was anxious to get on with it, to take up the platform, to get down to business, to finish in time, to adjourn and go home.

The timing and my nerves were getting tight, but even as the hours passed I didn't really doubt that our delegates would stick it out until the convention had concluded. And then, just as we were about to adjourn for lunch, every prospect suddenly changed.

It was such a trivial thing that did it ... just a routine little announcement. The Executive Secretary of the party, Jim Pederson, who was undoubtedly trying to be helpful, came up to the podium and waited with a worried look until the noise had settled down somewhat. Then he gave his warning message to the delegates: they mustn't forget the check-out time. They had to be out of their rooms by three o'clock, that was the official deadline. Furthermore, having just spoken with representatives of the hotel, he had to report that another convention was moving in this very evening. The present occupants of the rooms would simply have to be packed and out by three. "Please cooperate with the hotel because they have been good to us," Pederson advised.

His call for reciprocal courtesy was probably of limited appeal, but the threat of an extra day's room rent was something else again. The delegates were quickly stirred to action. Some left the hall at once. All about me I could hear the discussion of departure plans; people were talking about car pools and luggage racks and the length of the long ride home. Some were taking off their delegate badges and leaving them on their chairs, as sure a sign as any that for them this convention was over.

They would have preferred to stick it out until the real adjournment, of course. They knew very well that it would be better to stay. And they had no objection to discussing the platform. But time was running out. They were anxious to be on the road. They were nervous about the check-out time. They had to be back at work. Having sat through a day and a half of speeches, and taken part in the handful of critical votes, they were able to see their duty as being already largely discharged.

So they headed for the door even before the break for lunch, and in distressing numbers. Distressing to me, at any rate. Some of the McCarthy floor leaders looked exultant as they sensed that the ranks of the foe were thinning. They began to guess what could happen before the day was out.

The prospect was becoming clearer to me too. If the rate of departure continued much longer, it would be obvious to everyone that the old majority was no longer in control. It wasn't hard to imagine what the new majority would do once it recognized its advantage.

The really frustrating thing was that I couldn't think of anything to do about it. If our delegates wanted to go home, I didn't see how we could stop them. I felt helpless, resigned to simply watching them head for the door. Like a lemming, I fell in step and numbly joined the crowd.

When I reached the lobby I saw that others had been a good deal more resourceful than I. Outside each of the exits from the convention floor there were teams of our student volunteers. They were waiting for the delegates to come out through the doors. Each delegate was offered assistance in checking out of the hotel. A student would propose to do the whole job for him: go to his room, pack his suitcases, check the delegate out by three o'clock (he could pay his bill later), store his luggage in a safe place off the lobby, and deliver the claim check for it to him back on the floor. A surprising number of delegates were taking the students up on this offer. They were handing over their room keys and returning to their seats. The tide had been stemmed, at least for a while.

Disaster had been averted, but its possibility was clearer than ever before. If the consequences of our shrinking numerical superiority now seemed less imminent, they were considerably more vivid. My own apprehension was bordering on panic. The convention was moving too slowly. At best the debate on the platform would consume less time than it deserved. At worst, the walkout of our delegates would soon occur all over again. And next time around no friendly students would be able to stop them from leaving. Any further delay in the convention would be ruinous. Even the hour-long break for lunch, which was scheduled to begin very shortly, struck me as a senseless squandering of precious time.

It was just then, with the luncheon recess about to start, that I received an urgent message: I was to go at once to the McKnight Suite, on the top floor of the hotel, and meet there with Bill Connell, who had something very important to tell me. Connell, whom I knew only slightly, was Humphrey's administrative assistant, his top salaried aide, and it was widely assumed at the convention that he was empowered to speak for the Vice-President in his absence. I couldn't imagine what he wanted to see me about.

The McKnight Suite was so called because it was retained on an annual basis by William McKnight, Board Chairman of the Minnesota Mining Company. The suite was huge and it commanded a stunning view of the Mississippi River, but the furniture and other appointments, however plush, were unmistakably those of the Hilton chain. Humphrey had used the suite as his personal headquarters while staying at the hotel the day before. After he had left, however, Connell had just stayed on, and now the cavernous set of rooms had become Connell's headquarters for the duration of the convention.

As I passed through the foyer and into the living room I saw that Connell was not alone. Sitting at a table in the corner was a lady whom I recognized from her pictures as Mrs. Eugenie Anderson, former American Ambassador to Denmark and now Ambassador to the United Nations. I knew very little about her, a few disjointed facts: the titles she'd held, that she was from the Minnesota town of Red Wing and had been active in the DFL many years earlier, and that she had unsuccessfully fought Eugene McCarthy for the party's endorsement for the United States Senate seat which was up for grabs in 1958.

Mrs. Anderson and Connell came directly to the point. They

had been reading the proposed DFL platform plank on Vietnam, and they didn't like it at all. I think the word they used was "unacceptable." It was explained just why I'd been summoned before them. They wanted some "appropriate" changes made; I was ordered to have them substituted at once.

I was so surprised that at first I wasn't even angry. This request—this order—was hard to believe. Let me try to suggest what was involved. I had read the two Vietnam planks and felt that both were tributes to verbal vacuity. Caution and compromise had led to every line. This was particularly true of the Majority plank. In fact, and this, I guess, says it all, there was a heated debate among the delegates over whether there even *was* a Majority plank. The Humphrey supporters insisted at first that theirs should be called the "unity plank." The Chairman of the Platform and Resolutions Committee, in submitting the plank, described it as "an effort to achieve party harmony." At the same time, however, he did note that "we were not able to get all the members of the Platform Committee in support." And so the McCarthy delegates were introducing their own plank, and this led to another battle over nomenclature. Because if you are so insistent on the unity status of your resolution that you can't even bear to have it called a Majority position, then what on earth are you to call the dissenting plank? You can't call it the Minority plank, because a minority implies a majority, and a majority precludes unanimity. So a number of Humphrey delegates actually referred to the McCarthy plank as merely the "substitute motion." That's how far things had gone. Rancor had descended to absurdity.

The semantic dueling between the delegates seemed sufficiently ridiculous even at the time. Today it seems impossible. As I write these lines, in 1971, I have before me the two alternative planks. They seem now quite innocuous and, more to the point, very similar. They weren't that far apart. Each side had worded its position in terms sufficiently general to permit the other to support it. Both seemed to be in opposition to the war. The differences were relatively minor. There were some distinctions, of course. Had I been a delegate and permitted to vote, I would have supported the Minority plank, as Congressman Fraser had already agreed to do, because I found it closer to my antiwar views, though not nearly as strong. Today even the Pentagon would find much of it hawkish. Its notion of a big troop reduction was the withdrawal of 50,000 men.

In any event, what was bothering Mrs. Anderson and Bill Connell had nothing to do with the Minority plank. I doubt whether they'd even read it. No, what had them so excited was the Majority position itself. They thought it went too far. Connell pointed, for example, to a clause which said that "In an effort to move the Paris peace talks out of the current impasse, we recommend the withdrawal of a limited number of American troops." He seemed to regard this suggestion as wildly excessive. He said it simply could not be permitted.

I tried to demur. I said that the platform recommendation was scarcely very novel, even from within the Administration. The phrase "limited number" could be subject, if necessary, to the most narrow interpretation. I said I didn't think that it was really that significant.

Connell exchanged a smile with Mrs. Anderson and then both turned upon me identical condescending looks of the bemused, sadly tolerant, head-shaking variety. When Mrs. Anderson finally spoke, it was as if to a small child. Her voice was friendly, even lilting at times. She was trying very patiently to make me understand.

"Young man," she intoned, "there is a peace conference on in Paris. Those negotiations, I can tell you as a diplomat, are in a very delicate stage right now. We must do nothing to upset them. Can you imagine what the effect of a provision such as this would have upon Hanoi?"

Frankly, I could not. As hard as I tried, I simply could not find or hold the image of the North Vietnamese Presidium— or whatever they call it—huddled around a teletype, waiting breathlessly for the exact wording to be transmitted from the St. Paul Hilton. As tactfully as possible, I tried to convey my doubts about the global repercussions of our purely local vote.

I should have saved my breath. To them the matter was already settled. Even as I spoke I could see that they were absorbed in reading the next item in the plank. So I looked it over too.

Now here, I thought, is language that is beyond dispute. *Dispute!* It was almost beyond *comprehension*. It was the near-perfect crystallization of timidity in prose. In its entirety it read: "We encourage the acceptance in South Vietnam of a coalition government; however, we should not seek to impose upon South Vietnam a coalition government."

Connell laid down his copy of the platform and exhaled a weary sigh. He turned his eyes toward the ceiling, thereby missing those of his confrere, which were brimming with sympathetic indignation.

Apparently I'd missed the point. What had seemed to me insipid was to them a source of menace, an intolerable concession which would have the most far-reaching effects on international diplomacy. They read it as the blueprint for Communist domination of the South.

I tried to rally some arguments in opposition to this curious view. I asked them to look at the language. I pointed out that "encourage" was at most a mild verb, and qualified, if not contradicted, by the final phrase of the provision. I noted that the components of the coalition government had not even been described. There was no indication of who was to be included. I asked just what the problem was.

My question went unanswered. The pair was already at work on drafting substitute language. They were busy scribbling something on a piece of hotel stationery. The new wording was finally handed over to me, but my opinion of it was definitely not solicited. It was made very clear that my role was that of messenger, not critic. Nonetheless, I read what they had written, "We encourage the participation by all parties in the political life of North and South Vietnam and we uphold the inalienable right of all people to self-determination."

The original provision had been so insipid that I didn't much care that its substitute was even more so. That was the least of my concerns. The pretentious absorption with minutiae seemed pretty disgusting, I'll admit, but it was a relatively minor irritant. What really bothered me was the problem of time. The convention was now recessed for lunch; it was scheduled to go back into session at two o'clock. This left only a few precious hours remaining at best. In fact, it might already be too late: it was possible that many of our delegates would find this hour's recess a convenient time to leave. If we did still have a majority after everyone was reassembled, we certainly wouldn't have it for long. The debate on the platform would have to be curtailed. And here were two people calmly, casually ordering substitute motions as if we had all the time in the world, motions which would take at least an hour to pass on the convention floor; meaningless motions, silly nit-picking addenda, but vastly consumptive of our ever-shrinking time.

Angry and exasperated, I tried to explain the seriousness of the situation. I said that what they were asking me to do was going to take a lot of time. I described the desperate measures which we had taken already to keep our delegates from leaving. I told them what could happen if we were to lose our majority.

"Oh, don't worry," said the Ambassadress, with a dismissive wave of her hand. "Our delegates won't go home. I know our people. I know our good strong DFLers."

I doubted that. I mean, how *could* she know them? She didn't spend that much time within the state. She worked out of New York. It was clear that neither she nor Connell had the faintest notion of how close we were to losing the whole convention.

And no matter how hard I tried, I simply couldn't get across to them my own sense of furious urgency. Once again I described the precariousness of our position. I said that to devote time to these changes now was to risk everything. It was really very simple: our people were going home.

"I don't think that's going to be a problem," said Connell.

"How the hell would you know," I thought, but only had the courage to ask in muted form. In response I received a little lecture on how this was the Vice-President's home state, and any line of any resolution that we passed here would be subject to the widest scrutiny. Just think about that, I was told.

"That's just it," I exclaimed, sensing that I finally had a winning point. Speaking much too fast—the luncheon recess was almost over—I asked how it would look if Gene McCarthy won all the national convention delegates from the Vice-President's home state. "Just think about *that*," I said. They looked at me as if they weren't sure whether I was stupid or crazy.

Then, for the sake of argument, I shifted gears and agreed that there might indeed be time to make their changes. But that meant we'd have no chance to take up any other planks. I informed them that we had assured the other side that the human rights plank, too, would receive a full discussion. We couldn't adjourn without taking up human rights. It would look as if we were trying to duck the issue. It would look as if our views on it were different from those of the other side. It would confirm the worst suspicions of the McCarthy supporters in our state.

Connell said rather coolly that he would be responsible for whatever happened on the convention floor, as if my chief concern was over the ascription of blame. They indicated that the meeting was over. Mrs. Anderson stood up and repeated the orders for amendment. From the way she spoke I might have been someone from room service. Which, in a manner of speaking, I was. I wasn't being asked, I was being told. And if I refused to deliver their orders to our floor leaders, why, they'd just have to do it themselves. There was nothing left to say, and nothing left to do but go back down to the convention floor.

I won't attempt to describe my emotions, all of them variants on impotent rage, but they were mild compared to the reaction of our floor leaders when I told them about my meeting upstairs. Still, there was nothing we could do. Connell had passed the word himself. People thought he was speaking for the Vice-President. The discipline which we'd striven so arduously to maintain among our delegates caused them to accept without a public complaint these new instructions. It was awful.

To my amazement, almost all of our delegates had returned for the afternoon session. But they weren't very happy about it. Our bank of phones was already starting to ring with angry inquiries about how long this was going to take. The delegates were saying that if the convention wasn't over soon, they'd leave anyway. All I could tell them was to try to be patient.

Seldom has advice been given with less conviction. What had remained of my own patience was now gone for good. It was past two-thirty. I didn't see how we could possibly hold out. I was jumpy and angry and filled with real despair. Every time I saw a delegate even approach the back exit I imagined that he was leaving the hotel.

The most exasperating thing of all was that we still hadn't begun discussion of the platform—not Vietnam, not human rights, not even the last-minute substitutions. We hadn't even touched on it. Instead, there was a prolonged and rather ugly little squabble over whether or not to confirm the five national delegates from the First Congressional District. It all had to do with which of the rival Dakota County delegations ought to have been seated at the First District convention. I still don't know why the McCarthy delegates squandered so much time in debating this question. They certainly knew that they hadn't the votes to prevail. And even if their arguments were correct, the change in numbers would still have left a Humphrey majority in the First District. There was literally nothing to be gained by pursuing the matter any further, and there was everything to be lost. The speeches were rambling, all bombast and rhetoric. Didn't these people realize that their fulminations were displacing the discussion of the issue which had brought them to this place? It was almost pleasant to be able to shift my rage from the Humphrey minions to the McCarthy spokesmen. When were we ever going to take up the platform?

Not soon, apparently. When the First District issue had

finally been resolved—it turned out exactly as both sides had known it would—we still weren't ready for the major business of the day. Several other matters were to be taken up first. A representative of the convention's Black Caucus had asked to be heard, and he spoke very well, though at some length, on the general theme of injustice. Next it was urged from the floor that some kind of memorial remarks be delivered in memory of both Robert Kennedy and Martin Luther King. That request could not be denied either, and a minister in attendance was called upon to do the honors.

And then we came to the platform. The time was quarter to four. The first plank to be taken up was that on Vietnam. A McCarthy delegate moved that the Minority report be substituted for the Majority report, and the first set of speakers were those in favor of this motion.

This was their chance, however long postponed. Despite their loss of the delegate fight, here was the time when they might yet prevail. A number of Humphrey delegates were strongly opposed to the war. I thought it possible, even likely, that the Minority report would pass.

But then I heard those speeches made on behalf of the cause of peace. They were interspersed with insult. The Humphrey delegates were the repeated targets of ridicule, accusation, and disdain. What was the sense of a reference to the "obviously high-cholesterol, middle-aged Humphrey delegates"? Was that supposed to win support? And once again the speakers devoted much of their time to reviling the process of delegate selection; the Humphrey majority was said to be "determined to send delegates to Chicago who in no way represent the views of the people as manifested on March 5th in this state." I was standing near the podium and I could see the entire room, every delegation. This convention, right or wrong, *did* represent the views of the people as expressed on the night of March 5th. I looked around the room again. I saw the seven delegates who were representing my own ward. Six of them were in their seats, and Opperman was off in a corner talking to some men I didn't recognize who were wearing large press badges. Our seven delegates had been selected fairly. That whole evening came back to me. I looked further and found the Becker County delegation, the same divided group of six I'd seen elected in Detroit Lakes. That had been fair too; they hadn't been chosen through some ruse. I looked at other, larger delegations in the hall, some for Humphrey, some not, some mixed. All of them were here because of what had happened on March 5th. The process had been the same in every case. Why should a political minority assume that just because its cause is just, it can have failed to reach majority status only from fraud or chicanery? The right to compete is not the right to prevail. In fact, the reason this minority had not prevailed in Minnesota was being shown—repeated, in fact— by these speakers for the McCarthy plank, so busy now unleashing arrogant verbal salvos at precisely those delegates whose support they might otherwise have won.

The speeches were followed by a lengthy demonstration on the floor. It was not the usual kind of demonstration; it was quieter, more orderly, and vastly more effective than most. It was indeed a demonstration of allegiance to a cause, and it was true enough to the essence of that cause to constitute the finest moment of the convention.

But it could not erase the invective that had preceded it. On the one issue on which they might be flexible, the Humphrey delegates had been insulted back into the intransigence which had marked their other votes. It all seemed such a shame.

And it was disconcerting, too, that the McCarthy demonstrators seemed so impervious to time. I don't think that their demonstration could have altered many votes, and it did consume forty-five minutes that could never be replaced. It used up time that should have been spent in discussing other issues. I was standing near a corner of the hall, very close to the marchers, who were singing "We Shall Overcome" as they filed slowly past. Their progress was continually pausing and starting up again, and so I had the opportunity to chat with several of the marchers. Including the Doctor's Wife, whose eyes were aglow with the nobility of her cause, and who stopped to ask me, in an incredulous, pitying voice, "How *can* you not join us?" I was much inclined to ask her, "How *can* you squander so much time that really should be devoted to the civil rights plank?" But she wouldn't have listened, and so I said nothing at all.

When the demonstrators had returned to their seats, the debate on the platform was resumed. The substitute language that had been worked out upstairs was introduced now on the floor and was eventually accepted by the somewhat puzzled Humphrey delegates. They may have been influenced by the main speaker on behalf of the amendment, Ambassador Eugenie Anderson—she began by reminding the convention that the Paris peace talks were in progress and ended by warning that "everyone who has ever conducted negotiations of any kind knows that when you are in the midst of delicate negotiations you don't take any step of any kind which may weaken your own position." Her rank and her tone suggested to many that she knew much more about this than she dared let on. I must say this, she was effective. You should have heard the way she said "delicate negotiations." The delegates were most impressed.

Once the Humphrey supporters had accepted all the changes (the McCarthy delegates abstained from this vote), there still remained the basic paper ballot to be cast by the whole convention—the Majority Report, as amended, versus the Minority Report, for those who chose to call it that. While the printed ballot was being prepared, further debate was entertained. It was somewhat more moderate in tone than that which had preceded it. For once the merits of the reports were actually being discussed. Refreshingly, though much too late, the delegates addressed themselves to issues instead of each other.

But as these speeches continued on, the room seemed slowly to be emptying out. All the time and talk of amending the Majority plank had finally exhausted beyond revival the patience of the loyalists. The Humphrey delegates were leaving, and in devastating numbers. There was actually a line-up at the door. Heading toward it, I imagined for a moment that something might be done to reverse the flow. But that thought lasted only until I had reached the lobby. There it became all too clear that nothing could be done. The delegates were not just planning to leave; they were getting in their cars and driving away. There was plenty of effort to stop them. Our students were imploring them to stay, but with almost no success. The delegates had their luggage in hand and were well beyond dissuasion. It was half past five o'clock and they were going home.

I cursed both factions for allowing this to happen. I thought of the pomposity that had been permitted to prevail, the inanity of the platform changes, the arrogance of the speeches on the other side. Each had led to nothing but delay. And I thought most of all of how pleasant it would be if only I could go home now too and not have to face what was waiting back in the convention hall.

I didn't leave, but for a while at least I couldn't bring myself to return to the convention floor. I walked up to our command post on the mezzanine. I checked in with the guardians of our tableful of phones. They were frantic. For hours every call had been a plea to hurry things up and conclude the proceedings, and for hours all they'd been able to do was to beg their people to remain. By now they were almost afraid to keep their floor count up to date. The newest figures showed our margin of control as almost gone. Even the most loyal delegates had phoned from the floor to announce that they would stay to vote on the Vietnam plank, but not one moment longer.

And now that vote was taking place. The ballots were being distributed. To hundreds of delegates the exercise of this franchise was the signal for departure. They voted and then they left.

I didn't have to be on the floor to know what was going on. Our closed-circuit TV set showed the rows of empty chairs. Even without television, you could tell what was happening. You could tell by the faces of our men at the phones. For two days they'd kept a nearly perfect running count of just how many votes were in attendance on the floor. For two long days they'd charted the presence and the size of our margin of victory and now that margin had ceased to exist. Panicked calls were coming in from delegation leaders who reported that their people had gone home. In some delegations, there was no one left to call. Our workers sat around the table, not quite knowing what to do. The phones rang much less frequently now. It had become very quiet.

Everyone turned to the television screen. The picture and the sound were poor, and the camera range was limited too; all you could see was the area near the podium. But it was enough. From the angry gaveling and the noise and the swift movement of figures in front of the camera you could tell that there was something close to chaos on the floor. Chaos there and silence in our room; both signals of the same disruption.

Only two things could happen now, and either one was awful. The McCarthy delegates, looking around and seeing themselves in the majority, could vote to reverse all the proceedings of the last two days—and then select national convention delegates of their own. Scarcely very fair, but probably within the rules. The Humphrey side, on the other hand, could move at once to adjourn. This action might be justified in terms of self-defense, for it would preserve the votes of the real majority which had been sent from the caucuses to this state convention. But it would also appear to be an effort to avoid discussion of the human rights plank, which was next on the agenda. And this impression, however wrong in fact, would convince the McCarthy delegates that their rivals were probably racists and certainly cowards. This was the kind of choice which remained before the convention. I wondered which side would act first.

I soon had the answer from the closed-circuit screen. A voice from beyond the camera range was moving to adjourn. The Chair called for ayes and nays—in the general din and through the static of the set it was hard to tell just which was louder—and then he declared that the convention was adjourned.

There was a roar from the crowd and it turned my blood

cold. I'd never heard anything like that before. From hundreds of throats there came at once a single howl of total rage. It seemed to shake the room. And then I realized that this wasn't coming from our TV set, this was the real thing we were hearing—all the way from the basement of the hotel, a wave of deep and angry sound which seemed to come up through the floor. Even muffled as it was by distance it remained a frightening thing. I looked at the screen as if to see what sort of image could possibly match the measure of that sound. The black-and-white flickering picture showed waves lapping over the podium—waves which, as I took a sharper look, turned out to be people, an angry crowd which was rushing up to the rostrum and seemed fully capable of inundating it. Those who were up near the speaker's platform —the party officials, the presiding officers—were stepping back, as if to escape the foaming surge of protest.

Nothing would have surprised me then, except what actually happened. Incredibly enough, the waves subsided. Some order was restored. I guess the credit goes to Karl Grittner, the state Senator who was acting as chief parliamentarian for the Humphrey forces. The angry delegates were asking for a standing vote on adjournment, and Grittner not only supported this, but asked the Humphrey delegates to vote against adjournment too. Many did, and so the convention was still on. Then Grittner quickly moved that the human rights plank be taken up, but as a special order of business, and that on conclusion of that vote the convention would be automatically adjourned. His motion was carried by an audience obviously impressed that he had helped to bring the convention back to life. And of course it provided the Humphrey delegates with some protection against any last-minute tricks.

Someone asked whether human rights included civil liberties too. Grittner, speaking for the Humphrey forces, agreed that it did. So planks on both subjects were debated and passed, and the vote on each was virtually unanimous. When this work had been finished, the convention was again declared adjourned and, thanks to Grittner's earlier motion, this time the adjournment was good. A spirit of relative accord had been achieved in which reversal of the delegate votes was not even attempted by the McCarthy delegates. But that was due in part to pure blind luck and to Grittner's presence of mind.

And even so, no one would suggest that the McCarthy delegates had any reason to be happy. Just before adjournment the results of the Vietnam vote had been announced and here again the Humphrey forces had prevailed. The McCarthy delegates had won really nothing at all at this convention. They had only their losses to think about as they prepared to depart for home.

It was not these losses which made them so angry; I think most of them recognized that the balloting had been fair and representative of the party's will. The Humphrey margin had been well known for some months before the state convention. So I doubt that that convention's votes were the cause of the bitterness now. I think that what made the McCarthy supporters so resentful was largely their perception of the other side. I think they continued to see the Humphrey advocates as venal and insensitive and devious, as somehow opposed to reason and peace. If anything, this view had been intensified during the two days at the St. Paul Hilton.

My own resentment was not against this distorted image, but at the senseless and avoidable events which had given it credence in the eyes of the vanquished faction. How easy it should have been to leave a more accurate impression. The delegates on either side had much more in common than their suspicions of one another. Most of them had brought quite similar qualities to the convention: fairness, decency, a diffused but earnest adherence to principle. But neither would believe that of the other. The McCarthy delegates were pleased with the human rights plank that both sides had finally voted for, but how could they forget that there had also been an attempt to adjourn without taking this up at all? And how could they know that that adjournment was not intended to avoid an issue, but to prevent a trick? That it was an act of desperation, because precious time had already been shamelessly squandered.

The Humphrey delegates had bitter memories too. They had won all the votes, but they were far from pleased with the convention. They could not forget the insults and the imprecations which had been hurled at them for two long days. Speakers bordering on the hysterical had accused them of monstrous motives and sinister methods. Those speakers represented neither the highest nor the broadest sentiments in the McCarthy movement. I don't think they spoke for even the majority of their own convention delegates. But how were the Humphrey delegates to know this? They tended to judge an entire cause by its most preemptive spokesmen.

Almost everyone made this error and that was the major problem. For each side deserved much better spokesmen than it got. The cream did not rise to the top. The most visible leaders were all too often those who arrogated the spotlight to themselves. The delegates had been selected by the people, but their spokesmen were largely self-appointed.

Self-appointed, and remote from the best they chose to represent. Nothing had become so clear throughout that troubled year or during the last two days. Mrs. Anderson and Bill Connell had their counterparts in the McCarthy movement too. I've said before that the DFL is not run by political bosses. But it does have its interlopers, and the net effect of these, whatever their motives, was irreversibly calamitous.

I went upstairs to get my things and passed by the open door of the McKnight Suite. Inside, Bill Connell was holding court. A dozen or so delegates were sitting around in rapt attention as he told tales of his dealings with the great. He was telling his small audience all about the national campaign. He was glowing, as he dominated that borrowed room. He seemed to feel that a great victory had somehow already been won.

I could hear his voice as I went to get an elevator. I heard his voice, and I thought of Opperman. I thought of all the hopes which had been unleashed that year and of all the second-raters who had tried to exploit them.

Whose fault was it that the best people in politics were not the ones who were being heard? It was the fault of the best people, I suppose—those who turned out for one glorious night of caucus democracy and then never showed up again, abandoning things to the Oppermans and the Connells. Maybe it's asking too much, but the others really should have stayed around.

The newspaper accounts were as misleading as ever. If you hadn't been there and you wanted to know what had happened, you were forced to rely on the press for the story. And that, at best, was through a glass, darkly.

Very darkly, I'm afraid. And it wasn't just the local press. The Minneapolis papers weren't so bad. The *Star* did begin its account by asserting that "Supporters of Vice-President Hubert Humphrey easily rammed through slates" of national convention delegates, but I was long since prepared for loaded verbs, inaccurately modified. Rather par for the course. The McCarthy delegates to Chicago had been *elected* by three urban congressional district conventions. The Humphrey delegates had been *rammed through* the state convention. I knew that the distinction was entirely verbal. Each side had in fact done precisely the same thing: engaged in winner-take-all whenever possible. The stories were different only in the telling. But what really bothered me about the *Star*'s article was its early adverb. "Rammed" I could accept, it was just another example of the reporter's prejudice, but "easily" was something else again. It was a personal affront. It was a blithe denial of all our efforts, of all the planning, discipline, and anxiety that had marked the convention for us.

I don't know why I expected more accuracy in the out-of-town accounts. But I did, and so, questful as Diogenes, I headed for the downtown newsstand to see what the country's major papers had to say.

I started with the New York *Times*. I'd seen a *Times* reporter at the convention in St. Paul, so I assumed that the story would be detailed as well as accurate. It was neither. Right on the front page of the massive Sunday edition was a headline which heralded perfectly the theme of the article below, "McCarthy Backers Bitter." The story stated that the McCarthy delegates had asked to be given a share of the at-large delegates "proportionate to the strength shown in winning three district conventions." There was no mention of the fact that in those three district conventions the McCarthy delegates had refused to give a proportional share of the delegates to the Humphrey side, that all fifteen of those national delegates were solid McCarthy supporters.

Only two DFLers had been quoted in the article. The first was Robert Metcalf, a law student from the Sixth Ward and perhaps Opperman's closest political colleague. He was quoted as saying that the convention had been "closed," though nowhere in his statement, or anywhere else in the article, were the particulars of this closure ever specified.

The second DFLer was Vance Opperman, whose comments continued the theme of rejection. I wondered why the reporter hadn't interviewed anyone else. Perhaps he had, but they weren't included in the story. I didn't think that two Sixth Ward students, both former S.D.S. members, were necessarily a perfect microcosm of the Minnesota DFL, or even of its McCarthy supporters. I didn't recognize the by-line of the article and assumed that the reporter must have been new to his job.

But the Monday issue of the *Times* had another front-page story, the omissions of which could not be attributed to inexperience, since it was written by James Reston, who wrote that "In Connecticut and Minnesota this weekend, the McCarthy supporters demanded that the state convention delegates represent the true feeling of the states concerned, and they lost in both places." I don't know what test Reston used in determining "the true feeling of the states concerned," but in my own state it seemed to me that that feeling was fairly represented in the DFL delegation to Chicago. Humphrey had a majority of the delegates, but not all of them by any means. Every poll, every possible expression of public feeling, indicated that Humphrey was supported by the majority of DFLers—indeed, of all Minnesotans—and therefore should have had the majority of the delegates. The evidence suggested that the McCarthy percentage of the DFL delegates was an almost perfect reflection of the McCarthy support among DFL voters. But here was an article saying that the true feeling of the state had not been represented. And the article was by James Reston! It would be easy to say that Reston knows more about acupuncture than he does about Minnesota politics. Except that's not what I think. I think that James Reston is as good a political analyst as we're likely to get. So how could he possibly have come up with such unsupported, unsupportable conclusions? I was afraid I knew the answer. Because all analyses are dependent on their facts. And from what source do the facts accrue for a think-piece in the Monday *Times*? From the Sunday *Times*, apparently.

I'm sure that I sound unduly concerned with the national coverage of a small Midwestern convention. But I'm trying to describe the way I felt when I first saw that coverage, and the truth is that I was stunned. Because all the time that I'd been observing the garbled facts and vastly misleading emphasis in our local papers, I'd just *assumed*—the thought was very comforting—that somewhere the real story was going to be reported. And now I saw that the best reporter from the best paper in America was tackling the job and that the real story was eluding him too. If the New York *Times* wasn't going to get it right, then what other paper was likely to?

Not the Los Angeles *Times*, it soon became clear, as I read my way through the stack of out-of-town papers. The article there was by D. J. R. Bruckner, a columnist not without a following of his own, who informed his readers that "At the convention Saturday, the Humphrey supporters managed to outvote their numerical strength because they had seized control of the committees and because they were able to defeat McCarthyite efforts to establish a one-man, one-vote rule on the convention floor."

I was impressed that so much misinformation could be contained in a single sentence. It was a dazzling achievement. The phrase "outvote their numerical strength" was literally true but wildly misleading, absent any notation of the fact that the McCarthy supporters had just as clearly outvoted *their* numerical strength whenever they had the chance, and that the net result of this practice by both factions was a national delegation quite representative of the voters of the state. Each abuse had balanced off the other. Then there was our old friend, the loaded verb—in this case, "seized." In what possible sense had the Humphrey supporters "seized control of the committees"? Every committee was composed of two members from each of the eight congressional districts. Since the Humphrey supporters had carried five districts, and the McCarthy supporters three, each committee had the same ten-to-six split. If the First District had gone to McCarthy, as it very nearly did, each committee would have been tied at eight-to-eight. If the McCarthy supporters had won still another district, they would have controlled each committee by the same ten-to-six margin that the Humphrey delegates had in fact achieved. If this had happened, would Bruckner have written that the McCarthy delegates had "seized control of the committees"? I'm rather inclined to doubt it. My guess is that the verb would have been "won." Much more to the point (the point being the lapses of the press) was Bruckner's bland assumption that control of the committees had permitted one side to "outvote" their true strength on the floor. But that's not true. It simply has no basis in fact. And then there's Bruckner's final phrase, the charge that the Humphrey supporters had won by thwarting "McCarthyite efforts to establish a one-man, one-vote rule on the convention floor." I don't know what this means. There was no McCarthy floor effort to establish a one-man, one-vote rule. It's hard to figure what Bruckner had in mind. Perhaps he was referring to the question of whether each delegate's vote should be counted singly, or whether county strength should be used. Under the county strength rule, which was in effect at the convention, a county delegation of, say, six members was entitled to its full six votes even if only some of them were present on the floor. Regardless of the merits of this rule—employed by the McCarthy forces throughout the year—it surely offered no advantage to the Humphrey supporters. They had at all times maintained a clear numerical majority (a one-man, one-vote majority, if that's what one prefers to call it) and so never needed the conjectural advantage of a county-unit rule. That's probably why the McCarthy delegates never raised a challenge to this rule on the floor. A columnist in the Los Angeles *Times* was saying that they *did* bring such a challenge, and that the Humphrey supporters had defeated it, and that because they had defeated it they were able to prevail. This account of what transpired is wholly imaginary. It's just not true, as the transcript of the convention and the memories of its participants can attest. Yet it has become the truth, I guess, in some Orwellian way, for all those people who read all those stories in all those papers and in every case received the same misinformation. I wasn't surprised when *The New Republic* included Minnesota on its list of states whose conventions had been "railroaded." I suppose that it could have been worse.

It's not that our convention was above reproach. Both sides had earned some honest criticism. The Humphrey supporters, for example, had accepted without question those asinine last-minute changes in the Vietnam plank. The ease with which the substitute motion from upstairs had superceded the patient work of the convention committee was something that should have been reported. And there was the incontrovertible fact that the six-vote minimum then enjoyed by each county (and since abolished) did give an advantage to the rural forces. Not enough of an advantage to have altered the fair result, but an unearned advantage just the same, and so a proper subject of reportage, too. These things were fair game. But not things that never happened, not political tricks that never took place. Whatever else could be said about the Humphrey supporters at the convention in St. Paul, they had won their national delegates not through coercion or guile but simply because they had the majority of votes. I really wish the facts had been reported. It might have helped prevent what was to come.

10 Although I went to the Chicago convention—stayed at the Hilton there, right in the middle of that mess—what I seem to remember most vividly were the scenes that I saw on TV. Television sets were everywhere, and they were always on, not only in the hotel rooms, or even in the lobby, but in the amphitheater, too. Delegates continually stopped to stare at those sets, as if checking up on themselves. It was like a convention of actors, with plenty of mirrors around.

I watched the sets as avidly as anyone else. The small black-and-white picture seemed more a part of the real convention than the delegates who stood watching it. And what it showed was not only absorbing, it was new. The "real" convention, the live one, did not seem nearly that surprising or dramatic. By that time, nothing did. After midsummer, the rest of the year had just played itself out. The scope became national, and the voices louder, but there was nothing that one hadn't seen long before—omitting only the intrusion of physical violence, but even that was well rooted in the beginnings of the year, the expression, not the cause, of the spirit of the time, perfectly consistent with everything that had preceded it: the anger, the suspicion, the escalating rhetoric of hatred, the blindness of the leadership on either side. Not a very surprising end for a year that had started with a gun at a precinct caucus. Very much the same old story. Except when it became condensed and quickened, alarmingly intensified within the stark confines of those eighteen-inch screens. That was a new picture, all right, and impossible to forget. What little else I remember of Chicago seems very fragmented indeed.

I was not there as a delegate. I really had no role at all.

But our state Humphrey Chairman, Wendell Anderson, who *was* a delegate, thought that I would want to observe a national convention, and so had obtained for me, with considerable difficulty, a room at the Chicago Hilton, where the Minnesota delegation was staying.

I remember arriving at that room. In the humid chaos of the lobby I'd been unable to locate a bellboy, but did at least manage to get hold of my key. With this clenched between my teeth, and a suitcase in each hand, I traversed the length of the Hilton lobby, got in line for an elevator, sweated heavily, reached my floor, retraced my steps ten stories above their original route, and finally reached a door with the same number as my key. I went inside and before I'd even put my suitcases down I realized that the phone was ringing.

The voice was familiar. It was a man about my age, the former Hennepin County DFL staff man, the one who'd been replaced by the McCarthy girl from the Twelfth Ward. He was now working in the national Humphrey organization. He said he was assigned to what they called the "Delegate Section," headquartered somewhere in the same hotel. He came right to the point. They, by which I think he meant himself, since he was as new to this activity as I and probably desperate for help, wanted me to be the Humphrey man in charge of the South Dakota delegation.

I thanked him, but declined. It was not a difficult decision. All I knew about South Dakota was that it was west of Minnesota and that its delegates were probably supporting their Senator, George McGovern. I didn't know any of them and doubted whether even close acquaintance would have been of much help. I explained that I was in Chicago as an observer, and the response to this was one of clear resentment. By repeating my refusal three more times I was able finally to get off the phone.

The whole thing seemed very odd. I thought about it while I unpacked. This was the day before the start of the convention. It seemed awfully late in the game to be looking for extra staff—and specialized staff at that. I should have thought that a South Dakotan would be holding the job I'd just been offered. Someone who knew the members of that delegation. I really didn't see what a total stranger could accomplish. It seemed a very casual way to try to win a convention. Not a bit like the months of careful preparation for our state convention in St. Paul.

Just as I was putting away the last of my things, with a growing damp awareness that the air-conditioning didn't seem to work, the phone began to ring again. It was from the same office, but this time a different voice. And a different offer. I was asked to be in charge of the Wisconsin delegation. The tone of the request was pleasantly respectful, as if in tribute to my shrewdness at turning down a lesser spot. That's really what they thought: that I'd been bargaining. The Wisconsin delegation was much larger than South Dakota's. It was just assumed that I had held out for the best that I could get. In fact, when once again I had asserted my observer status I could almost hear my caller trying to think of just what job I would finally be willing to settle for. I hung up and decided to shower and change before looking for some friends in the hotel.

It wasn't long before the phone had started in again. This time the offer was expressed in guarded tones. Nothing was being definitely extended, I was led to understand, but how would I feel about sharing the California assignment with just one other person?

I was impressed. They didn't even have a man for California yet. *California.* What incompetence. Whoever eventually did accept any of these escalating offers was going to have to spend all of his time with the state delegation to which he'd been assigned. He'd be expected to eat with those delegates, drink with them, listen in at their meetings, and hover near them on the floor of the convention itself. His job was to win them over, to lure even a few delegates into the Humphrey fold. Now, how can you change the political convictions of people you don't even know? How do you know who might be susceptible? Where do you start? *When* do you start? Surely not the day before the convention. It made me think of another Hilton, back in St. Paul, and of the ponderous, tardy machinations of Bill Connell and Eugenie Anderson. I wondered if they were working in the Delegate Section here.

The easiest way to avoid my phone was simply to leave the room. Heading down the hall I passed several members of the Minnesota delegation who were having as much trouble as I in finding their way back to the elevators. There were so many corridors, and each seemed to end in a cul-de-sac. Our mutual confusion made conversation easier—sometimes imperative—between people who'd been enemies since the caucuses back home. I ran into Howie Kaibel and his wife, Ronnie, whose room was just down the hall from mine. They were relatively friendly. Howie said he'd been assigned to cover the Canal Zone for the McCarthy camp. I congratulated him, and though I did refrain from mentioning either California or Wisconsin, I couldn't resist at least telling Howie that I had just recently been offered South Dakota. I didn't want to overdo it. We were like kids with baseball trading cards. I thought I'd save the big ones for a more appropriate swap.

Howie was taking his assignment very seriously. You couldn't fault his dedication. I'd been revising my opinion of Howie since our first encounter at the meeting of the newly captured Sixth Ward club. Throughout the following months it had become increasingly clear that Howie Kaibel was not Vance Opperman. I think that what kept him going was a heartfelt desire to end the war. And, to my surprise, what also had come through was his allegiance to party politics. He really believed in our political system. He believed in broad coalitions that had the clout to get things done. That his actions had helped to frustrate his goals, had shattered our own DFL coalition, and rendered the peace movement locally ineffective were tragedies of inexperience and not of ambition. I wished him well with his convention task.

Several frazzled Minnesotans whom I met in the hall warned me that the lobby was a madhouse, and so I took the elevator up to the top of the hotel, getting out on the twenty-third floor. This, I had been told, was the command post of the Humphrey headquarters. The elevator opened onto a mini-lobby just like the ones on every other floor below, except that it was crowded with perspiring people and with what looked like photographic equipment. And there were policemen stationed at the corners of the room. You couldn't leave the foyer unless you had a badge. Since the place where one might get a badge was somewhere beyond the foyer, it looked as if I would get no further on that floor. But then I spotted a good friend, Paul Thatcher, whose wife Margee I had unsuccessfully nominated for Hennepin County Chairwoman. Paul, I could see, was wearing a badge; in fact, several of them. I called out and got his attention.

It was amazing the way that Paul was able to wave me past those guards. As a favor to his friend, Senator Mondale, he was serving as head of Mondale's convention staff. This was a rather demanding job, since Mondale was the co-chairman of the national Humphrey campaign. Together we went back through winding halls, Paul stopping to vouch for me whenever a policeman halted our progress. We finally came to a door that was guarded like a vault, and were able, after further words from Paul, to enter into a small workroom where I recognized several of my former co-workers from Mondale's Senate office. We went through two more doors and finally ended up in a very impressive suite. The view of the lake was spectacular. We were the only ones in those inner rooms, and the silence was a blessing after the tumult in the halls. Paul looked through several drawers and finally came up with a badge, a plastic rectangle about the size of a playing card, attached to a long cord which one wore around the neck. These badges were for the "official Humphrey staff." Each of them was numbered with large black numerals on its face. My number was 003, which I found most impressive until Paul explained that the badges had been given out in descending numerical order. There were only two of them left.

I was delighted to have one. If I ran into any further scouts from the Delegate Section, the plastic card suspended on my chest would give credence to my excuse that I was otherwise engaged. Now I really could be an observer.

If I could get around, that is. Even before the convention

had begun, mobility had virtually ceased. The Chicago Hilton is the largest hotel in the world but even its cavernous space had been innundated past endurance. Everyone was jammed together and nothing worked at all.

I waited almost half an hour to get an elevator down from the twenty-third floor, and then stepped out into a lobby that was impossibly overcrowded. It was no good trying to walk around. You could hardly move. So I stood by a pillar and watched the crowd pass by en masse, a sweltering procession which moved along by congregate fits and starts.

And what a procession. Only a wry or malevolent fate would have decreed that such diversity be packed so closely together. The conjunction was astounding. Every age and every rage of the national ferment could be seen.

I found that I recognized a number of the passing faces. And not just the celebrities, either. There were people whom I hadn't seen since childhood. The whole populace of my memory seemed to have turned out. Neighbors, classmates, people I'd worked with in Washington, casual acquaintances from every part of the country and from every stage of my past. As I stood there by my pillar I thought of the line about Shepheard's Hotel, where everyone you ever knew would eventually pass by. The intensity of the heat made the comparison that much easier. I stayed where I was and greeted those I knew, as each in turned inched slowly by.

I saw a law school classmate who claimed that I owed him a drink. I saw a man that I'd met in New York who did owe me a cigar. I was just barely able to recognize, in sandals, beard, and cloak, the ablest of the bright young men whose government career had seemed so certain in Washington two years earlier. I saw a political science professor whom I'd always assumed was a McCarthy supporter, and he stopped to relate with evident pride that he'd just been asked to cover the Wisconsin delegation for Humphrey. A national lobbyist came over to add that he would be handling South Dakota.

A number of those I recognized were young friends from the Sixth Ward. I saw Joel, and Jock, and a good many others, who had driven or hitchhiked to Chicago. They weren't really part of any particular organized group. They just wanted to be there, to see what was going on. They were observers, like me. And equally bewildered by the crush and the heat of the crowd.

I ended up spending much of the convention with them. We ate together frequently and went to see the demonstrators who were gathering in the park. I've said that my sharpest impressions of the Chicago convention were those I received from TV, and they were, but much of the rest that now comes to mind were the scenes that I shared with the Sixth Ward students, in whose company, it seems, I was ordained to spend the year.

I was with them, for example, on the opening night of the convention. I didn't have a visitor's pass, and so had stayed behind to watch the session from the hotel. But my television set was on the blink (*nothing* seemed to work), and so I went down the hall to the Kaibel's room and asked if I could watch with the people who were there. The room was pretty full. Most of the Sixth Ward visitors to Chicago could not afford hotels, and some had been invited to spend the night on Kaibel's floor. Others had stopped in to watch the convention on TV. I found a vacant spot on the floor by the set and tried to follow the proceedings between the commercials. It wasn't easy. As the only non-McCarthy supporter in the room, I was subject to a number of comments, only some of them good-natured. Ronnie Kaibel was particularly severe. I had to listen to a long harangue about the failure of the democratic process, about the total domination of the venal party bosses. She made it very clear that I was one of those to whom she was referring, a usurper of the power that the people ought to have. I tried to point out that if I was a party boss I wasn't a very good one, since, like them, I could get no closer to the convention than to watch it on TV. And what I had been watching there was Ronnie's husband Howie, who as a Minnesota delegate kept bobbing into view. "That," she retorted, "is the exception that proves the rule."

I don't blame them for being suspicious. My credibility, such as it had been with them, was wiped out completely by the flashy plastic badge that I was wearing around my neck. It really didn't matter much whatever I chose to say; I was known as 003 to the students in that room.

And it's not that I thought that their resentment was unfounded. It just wasn't directed at quite the proper place. It was very clear that many states had not selected their delegates with anything like the standards that had prevailed in Minnesota. And it was true that at this national convention the arrangements, the logistics, the machinery if you will, were very tightly controlled by just one man. But that man wasn't Humphrey; it was clearly Lyndon Johnson.

There was no question of the omnipresence of The Man Who Wasn't There. Johnson's remote control influence was simply assumed by most of the Humphrey camp. I'd seen a good example at firsthand. I had been back on the twenty-third floor, visiting with Paul Thatcher, when Mondale came in with a group of constituents who wanted passes to the visitor's gallery for one of the sessions of the convention. The constituents were all active DFLers, and they were pretty insistent that they get those passes. They refused to believe that Mondale couldn't help them. He was, after all, one of the chairmen of Humphrey's pre-endorsement campaign. They couldn't believe that he couldn't get a couple of passes if he really chose to try. But the fact is that he couldn't. The passes—all such matters—were in the hands of the Johnson representative down the hall. And he was holding on to them, for purposes of his own. Mondale made a number of calls, but there was no one who could help. The problem was finally solved by Warren Spannaus, the DFL State Chairman. On a trip to Washington he had struck up a friendship with Sam Houston Johnson, the President's brother. Acting on a hunch now, Spannaus put through a call to Sam Houston back at the ranch. Within an hour, the Minnesotans had their tickets—and an indelible demonstration of just who was completely in charge.

As each day of that ghastly convention progressed, the resentment of the students plainly grew, and with it the distance between us. We continued to spend some time together, but they no longer wanted to listen, and I was having trouble in finding what to say. It was difficult to express to my angry and impatient friends just what I thought were truly the sources of the tragedy of that year. When I tried to put it into words, my explanation seemed too simple. Too simple, and too lengthy as well, because I wanted to review the whole course of the year. I wanted them to know that everything that was happening now was related to everything that had happened before, to the events that we had seen together, to all the little failures that had defeated the largest hopes. How could I tell them that they had known the truth at the beginning of the year, but that they didn't know it now? That they had been right to proceed as the civics books directed, to turn out and organize in all the Sixth Wards of the land. That if this tactic didn't work, it was because not enough had worked at it; it was because the worst among them had subordinated their cause for gain.

And how could I possibly tell them, then, that they had started much too late. This seemed to me the very essence of the problem. To work within a political party does not mean raiding it on occasion, no matter how noble the cause. It's got to be a regular thing. To ring doorbells in New Hampshire for several weeks is admirable, but to ring them over a period of years, back in one's own ward, is really what counts. Consistent participation in a political party is the only form of leverage that can truly change events. Yet those who ring doorbells for three weeks are called heroes, and those who work much longer are invariably known as hacks. How could I, in the midst of the Chicago convention, inform my young, disillusioned friends that what they really ought to be was just such party hacks? How corny that would sound to them, how hopelessly out-of-date. So just imagine what they would have thought about this further point of view: that if the good people of this country had been in the habit of attending ward club meetings once a month, the disasters of 1968 need never have happened at all. Not the Chicago convention, not the violence, not the hatred, not the sundering of the nation's largest coalition. Perhaps not even the war in Vietnam. For no politician, no president, no national or state leader, could ever withstand a party whose members cared enough to go to ward club meetings once a month. That's really all it would take. But most people aren't willing to do even that much, no matter what they say. It would take so little to change things, but they don't seem ready to try. So the Oppermans and Connells take over and fill the political void. But the only way they can do so is through better people's default.

As I say, the Chicago convention was not really the place to point these things out to young listeners. I never even tried. But someone else did. Let me share with you that final memory, at the close of that awful convention.

It was four o'clock in the morning and I was sound asleep, oblivious at last to the angry chants from the crowd outside my window. I don't know how long the phone had been ringing, but it finally woke me up. It was Paul, apparently tireless, still at work on the twenty-third floor.

"David," he said, "who's the Chairman of the Sixth Ward Club?"

I asked him if he knew what time it was.

"Listen, fella," he said, "Isn't that your ward club? Who's the Chairman?"

"Vance Opperman. No, wait a minute. He resigned when he became County Chairman. I think it's Howie Kaibel now. Why do you want to know?"

"Get over to your window and you'll find out. There's a guy out there in Grant Park who's giving some kind of a speech, and he keeps saying that he's the Chairman of the Sixth Ward club. In Minneapolis."

"What else is he saying?"

"I can't hear very well, we're up too high. But he's got himself quite a crowd."

I hung up the phone and jumped out of bed, right onto the arm of a graduate student from the ward club whom I was letting spend the night on the floor. It didn't seem to bother him, at least he didn't wake up. I went over to the window and leaned out. There *was* a commotion in the park across from the hotel. I mean a specific commotion, not just the general disorder of the last few days. There was a speaker on some sort of platform, surrounded by a crowd of young protesters, some of whom were by this time wearing bandages. They were shouting things at him. They seemed to be angry at whatever he was saying. I squinted at the figure who was speaking in the park. It was Howie Kaibel, all right.

Howie was delivering a political speech. And as I listened I knew why the protesters were angry. He couldn't possibly have picked a less acceptable theme for that crowd. The views he was expressing were as unfashionable as mine. He was exhorting his listeners to return to the political process. He was telling them that the system could work. He was pleading with them to go back to their communities and start organizing there to take over their local parties. He assured them that he knew it could be done.

I'm afraid they weren't buying it. And they didn't hide their scorn. Epithets were hurled out into the floodlit night. There's really no point in cataloging too precisely the abuse; suffice to say that the idiom was earthy.

But Howie stood there and took it. He insisted on continuing his talk. The shouts from the crowd of his contemporaries were getting louder, but Howie had some sort of microphone and so managed to be heard. He was talking now about the Sixth Ward club, about how students had taken over a county. He was wearing his national delegate's badge. "If we could do it, you can do it, too," he cried.

Loud moans and boos drowned out his further words. At least I couldn't hear them from my room. I listened to the mounting roar of disapproval. They were calling him a traitor. But Howie kept on speaking. I could see him gesturing desperately to that increasingly stormy crowd.

I shut the window slowly and walked carefully back to bed. I didn't want to wake the student who was sleeping on the floor. It took me awhile to get to sleep myself. I felt sorry for Howie, who was having a rough time out there in the park. I felt sorry for all the rest of us, who were having a rough time of it, too. And I wondered if things would ever get better, and when.

Same theme - describe [party?]

Johnsons resignation as result of McCarthy movement - shows effecting of system to respond